THE PLANETS

THE PLANETS

A Journey Into Space

Eric Flaum

CRESCENT BOOKS
New York

A FRIEDMAN GROUP BOOK

Copyright © 1988 by Michael Friedman Publishing Group, Inc.

This 1988 edition published by Crescent Books,
distributed by Crown Publishers, Inc.
225 Park Avenue South,
New York, New York 10003.

Library of Congress Cataloging-in-Publication Data

Flaum, Eric.
The planets.

1.Planets—Photographs from space.   2. Planets—Photographs.   I. Title.
QB595.F58   1988   523.4'9   88-3995

ISBN 0-517-66175-6

THE PLANETS
was prepared and produced by
Michael Friedman Publishing Group, Inc.
15 West 26th Street
New York, New York 10010

Editor: Sharon Kalman
Art Director: Mary Moriarty
Designer: Marcena J. Mulford
Photo Editor: Christopher Bain
Production Manager: Karen L. Greenberg

Printed and bound in Hong Kong by South China Printing Co.

To Seija—the center of my own solar system

ACKNOWLEDGMENTS

My Grandfather took me to the planetarium when I was a
child. We watched the lights move across the domed
ceiling, and afterwards looked at pictures of distant galaxies.
Since that time, I have looked to the sky with wonder.
Later I shared an eyepiece with my father, sighting planets
through condensed breaths on cold nights. We discovered
ringed Saturn, the lunar valleys, and the Galilean moons.
Without these two men this book may still have been
possible, but it wouldn't have been nearly as much fun!

Karla (AF), for the opportunity and the confidence, the
care and the concern

Alison (AV), for her friendship and enthusiasm; my favorite
earthnocentric with the right words at the right time

Tim and Sharon for their infinite—ok,
interstellar—patience through surgery, stickers, and
ridiculously late submissions

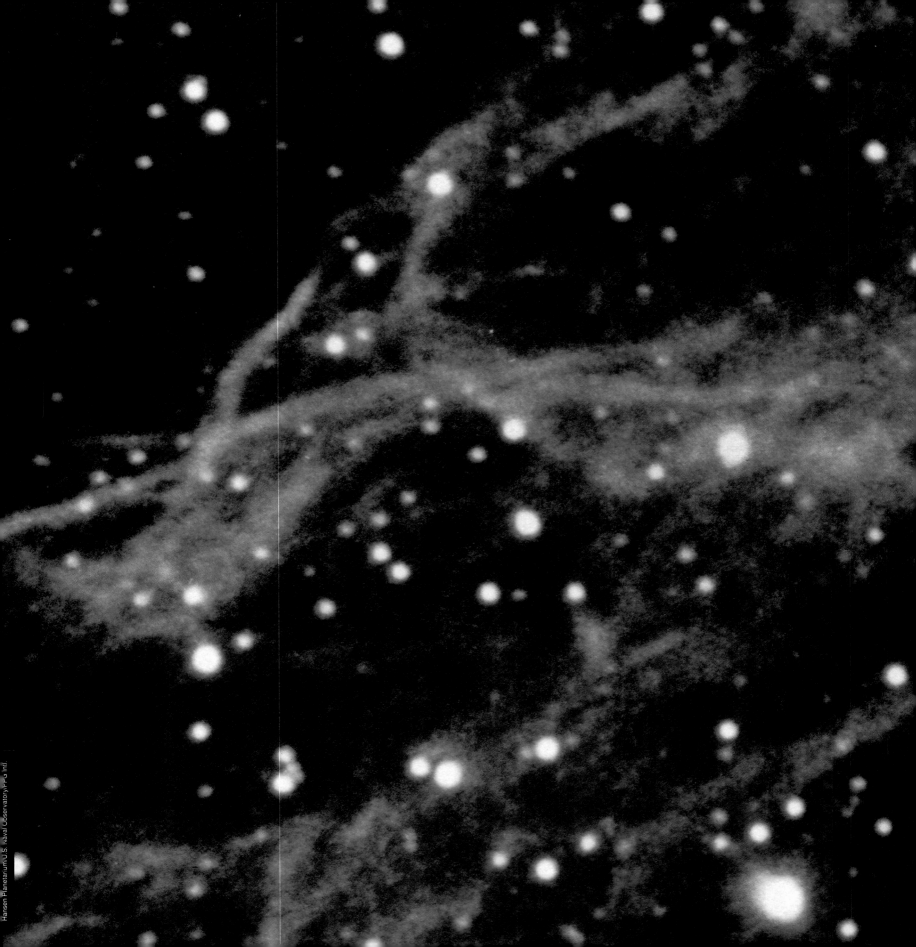

CONTENTS

INTRODUCTION

*"The particle and the planet are subject to the same laws,
and what is learned of one will be known of the other."*

—James Smithson
1765–1829

From our perspective here on Earth, the solar system is a truly enormous place. Great distances separate even the closest planetary neighbors. Though we once thought ourselves to be the very center of the Universe, we now understand our place as a rather undistinguished little member of an incomprehensible brotherhood of stars and galaxies. Despite the misconceptions of early theorists, our solar system is merely a small part in a much greater picture that still eludes our understanding.

Since Galileo first trained a telescope on the Moon, the science of astronomy has grown by leaps and bounds. Working with physicists and mathematicians, geologists and chemists, astronomers have developed a picture of the planets that is rich in detail and description. Though readily admitting to a great number of unanswered questions, astronomers have nonetheless filled in many of the uncertainties of those who have looked up to the night sky in wonder.

When the founder of the Smithsonian Institute uttered the above quote, Uranus had just recently been sighted, ushering in a new era of planetary science. From this, astronomers learned that our solar system was four times the size that they had originally thought. It also lead to the discovery of two other new planets: Neptune and Pluto. Some astronomers still continue to gaze farther out, hoping to extend our neighborhood even more.

The Sun itself is responsible for the very existence of its minute satellites, and serves as an enormous canvas against which the planets are a dazzling assortment of colors. Each leaves its own distant "fingerprint," a streak of motion across the relative emptiness of interplanetary space. In recent years, a number of earthly interlopers have streaked through that emptiness as well. Along the way, such probes have managed to send a great deal of information back to the earthlings that created them.

Celebrated missions and obscure experiments have made the last few decades the most exciting of all in planetary science. New information arrives each year, month, day. Theories are confirmed or dispelled, creating still newer theories in their wake. As this is written, and as it is read, on this planet and across space, we are learning more about our own neighbors, and in doing so are learning more about ourselves. Only in looking out can we ever see in. As we focus our gaze on the planets, the particles around us become clearer, too.

© Mike Chuang/FPG Intl.

The SUN

IN THE BEGINNING THERE WAS CHAOS, WHERE MATTER FLOATED FREELY THROUGH SPACE. WITH the passage of time, for reasons still not entirely clear to us, our galaxy came to be. Over the course of its formation, the matter collected into great clouds from which proto-stars came into existence. Back then everything around was in a "proto-" stage. Chance pockets of matter attracted more matter, gaining momentum as they went along. Though not discovered by earthlings for another five billion years, gravity was nonetheless hard at work. It increased exponentially, forming an enormous concentration of matter.

Around this time, the coalescing stellar cloud that would eventually form our Sun extended as far as Neptune's current orbit. This cloud was a spinning disc, its center becoming increasingly compact, while its outer regions began to break up into what would ultimately become the planets. As the temperature and pressure at the proto-star's center grew, its gravitational attraction increased as well. Some four and one half billion years ago enough of this matter came together to create what is now known as the Sun. When excited by temperatures above 10,000,000 K (Kelvin), atoms of hydrogen began to collide so fast that they produced enough energy to ignite an enormous nuclear reactor. At the Sun's center, temperatures of millions of degrees turned hydrogen into helium. The newly created helium by-product worked its way through the layers of the twisting orb, spreading out like water from a spinning lawn sprinkler.

In the long history of the known galaxy, the planets are relative newcomers. Viewed objectively, they are insignificant impurities trapped along the outer edge of a fairly average star. That star accounts for nearly all of the matter in our solar system—an overwhelming ninety-nine percent. In some ways, the planets themselves could actually be considered parts of the Sun, clots of spent fuel and waste dangling precariously at its fringes. One astronomer dismissed them as "a mere by-product of gaseous nebulae," while another labeled them "microscopic impurities in the vast cosmic vacuum that surrounds our star."

Given our current understanding of the solar system, it seems quite incredible that just four hundred years ago men were jailed and their reputations ruined for upholding their belief in a heliocentric universe, which held the Sun at its center. Although Nicholas Copernicus reintroduced this theory in 1543, it had actually been considered and preserved in writing long before. In the third century B.C., Aristarchus of Samos is said to have proclaimed that the Sun and the stars were fixed in space, while Earth and the other planets moved around the Sun. Unfortunately, most of Aristarchus' friends didn't agree with him, and his model of the solar system was quickly dismissed. Dismissed, in fact, to the extent that none of Aristarchus' own writings have survived. It is only through references in a passage by Archimedes, himself a great mathematician, physicist, and inventor, that we know of Aristarchus' theories today. While Copernicus deserves great credit for his discoveries (as opposed to the *hypotheses* of the ancient Greeks), it is worth noting that he was not the first to imagine a heliocentric universe.

Like this distant galaxy (left), our own formed from a spinning cloud of matter. Each bright light in this photograph represents a history of creation as complex and fascinating as that of our Sun's.

Nicholas Copernicus, 1473–1543, is called the father of modern astronomy. His understanding of the true nature of our solar system paved the way for all who followed.

Until Copernicus' ideas finally took hold, mankind assumed the presence of a divine hand in the creation of the earth-based cosmos. It was necessary for scientific minds to accept the Sun as the center of the solar system before they could even begin to question the physical nature of its origins. Once underway, they quickly began to develop the theories we rely on today when we consider the formation of our Sun and the planets that surround it. The most popular current theory is actually one that was first proposed several centuries ago. Today, we believe that the German philosopher Immanuel Kant had the right general idea when he presented the concept of a solar system formed from a proto-solar nebula condensing into the Sun and a great many planetesimals.

In 1796, shortly after Kant presented his theory, a French mathematician, the Marquis de Laplace, proposed a similar yet more detailed cosmogony, which he called his nebular hypothesis. Earlier in this century some theorists believed that a specific force would have been needed to trigger the nebula's formation, such as a nearby supernova (an exploded star which emits great amounts of radiation and matter), but observations of fledgling star systems within our galaxy indicate that star birth can take place without such a catalyst.

Originally, the proto-Sun and its fledgling planets were connected by enormous clouds of loose matter. Eventually, most of this matter would be drawn into the creation of the Sun, while the outer pockets, sufficiently distant from the proto-Sun, created their own independent centers of gravity. The remarkably synchronized relationships found throughout our solar system seem to indicate a similar origin for all of the planets. The fact that all of their orbits match the rotation of the Sun is probably not a coincidence; only Venus' retrograde rotation denies uniformity in this area.

While such theories make sense to our modern scientific understanding, they still battle man's centuries-old perceptions of our solar system as a collection of neat, well-defined entities. The original view of the planets as tidy spheres making their way precisely around the Sun no longer agrees with scientific understanding, but dies hard in man's imagination. The complex interactions of forces between the Sun and the planets are not perfectly clear-cut. Pluto's questionable status as a planet and the micro-systems that surround Jupiter and Saturn are perfect examples of the fuzzy boundaries astronomers have come to accept.

Before proceeding to any examination of the planets, however, it is essential to possess an understanding of the Sun. No single body has a greater effect on Earth and its fellow planets. The Sun brought together the matter that first formed the planets, holds them in their orbits, and provides them with energy they could not possibly create on their own.

The Sun is actually a fairly typical member of the stellar population. Its magnitude (a measurement of an object's relative brightness) places it close to the stellar average, as does its classification as a yellow dwarf—an ordinary star in the prime of its life, undergoing the steady conversion of hydrogen into helium at its center. In the center, too, is a cauldron of thermonuclear fusion (the transformation of atomic nuclei into heavier elements brought about by great temperatures) creating temperatures as high as fifteen to twenty million degrees. Even at its surface, a mere six thousand degrees, the Sun is still so hot that everything on it immediately turns to gas.

Once ignited (see page 13), the Sun quickly expelled much of the uncontrolled dust and gas throughout the solar system. This cleansing process is known as a T Tauri wind, based on observations of young stars found in the constellation of Taurus, which many astronomers believe to be similar to our own Sun in its earliest stages. The T Tauri winds cleaned at least half a sun's worth of matter into interstellar space. The solar winds that currently buffet the earth are mild in comparison to the hurricane forces necessary to perform such a task. The completion of that solar housekeeping seems to have severed the final vestiges of the planets' direct attachment to the Sun. Though still inexorably bound to its gravitational force, they were no longer as completely surrounded by its outer mist.

Now, what is left is a Sun twisting slowly at the center of the solar system. (It should be noted that the T Tauri wind also created a braking effect on the Sun itself, slowing it down towards its current rate of rotation, about twenty-four to twenty-eight days.) While many of the planets would undergo further change through internal and atmospheric forces, the Sun itself has

This artist's rendering shows the orbits of the planets around the Sun. Comets swing in close before moving billions of kilometers away, and the asteroid belt forms an uncertain boundary between the inner and outer planets. To the left is a comparison of the planets' size in relation to the Sun.

PLUTO

NEPTUNE

URANUS

SATURN

JUPITER

MARS
EARTH
VENUS

MERCURY

"Let there be lights in the expanse of the sky to separate the day from the night, and let them serve as signs to mark seasons and days and years..."
—**The Book of Genesis**

changed little since then. Though its external activities are massive when compared to any planetary phenomena, they are actually the minor rumblings of an insatiable nuclear inferno.

We see the Sun as a steadily blazing ball of fire in our daytime sky, but it is actually a living force. Despite having settled into a fairly stable condition that should last eight or nine billion years, its inner machinations have been found to fluctuate over vastly shorter periods, such as the eleven-year solar sunspot cycle first discovered in the nineteenth century. (A combined Japanese and American mission will be launched shortly to study such peaks in solar activity expected around 1991.) Longer cycles extending over the course of several centuries are believed to have been responsible for climatic trends here on Earth, though direct study of these trends remains too recent to offer any conclusive evidence. Recently, a complex relationship between solar activity and the prevailing winds in the earth's stratosphere seemed to indicate such an interaction. While the information gathered is not sufficient for us to predict such trends, it remains an important step in our understanding of the Sun's effect on the planets. "So far this is statistical," said one of the atmospheric scientists involved. "We haven't explained it—we've only described it."

Most fascinating of all, though still largely unproven, is a theory recently formulated by those studying the extinction of past species on Earth. A number of proponents have emerged suggesting the existence of a twenty-six-million year cycle, at which intervals great numbers of species seem to have met their demise. Startlingly, certain scenarios for this cycle suggest the existence of a companion star to the Sun that travels in a long elliptical orbit similar to those long-period comets. A systematic search has begun for what would have to be a dim binary companion (in which two objects revolve around one another) for astronomers not to have noticed it earlier. The astronomers involved are particularly mindful of the fact that at least two-thirds of all known stars belong to double-star systems.

Despite its great mass and density, the Sun is composed entirely of gasses. The incredible pressure exerted on its core is enough to turn most matter to a liquid or solid state, were it not for the extremely high internal temperatures that exist. As a result, the Sun's radioactive zone (the area around the core) is a complex network of gaseous movement similar to the tradewinds of our own atmosphere. While the exact process remains unclear, the variations in density and temperature caused by the Sun's churning action are seen as being largely responsible for the fact that the Sun rotates faster at its center than it does towards the poles. Further away from the quickly spinning core, the Sun's outer layers lag behind.

These outer layers are made up of a plasma which itself possesses no electrical charge, yet serves as a superb conductant to either positive or negative charges. As a result, solar plasma closely interacts with the Sun's magnetic field. This interaction creates distortions in the magnetic field which form pockets of energy that build up and then manifest themselves at the surface as coronal holes (the portion of the Sun visible during a solar eclipse) and solar flares. This kind of activity has provided us with more information about the Sun than has anything else.

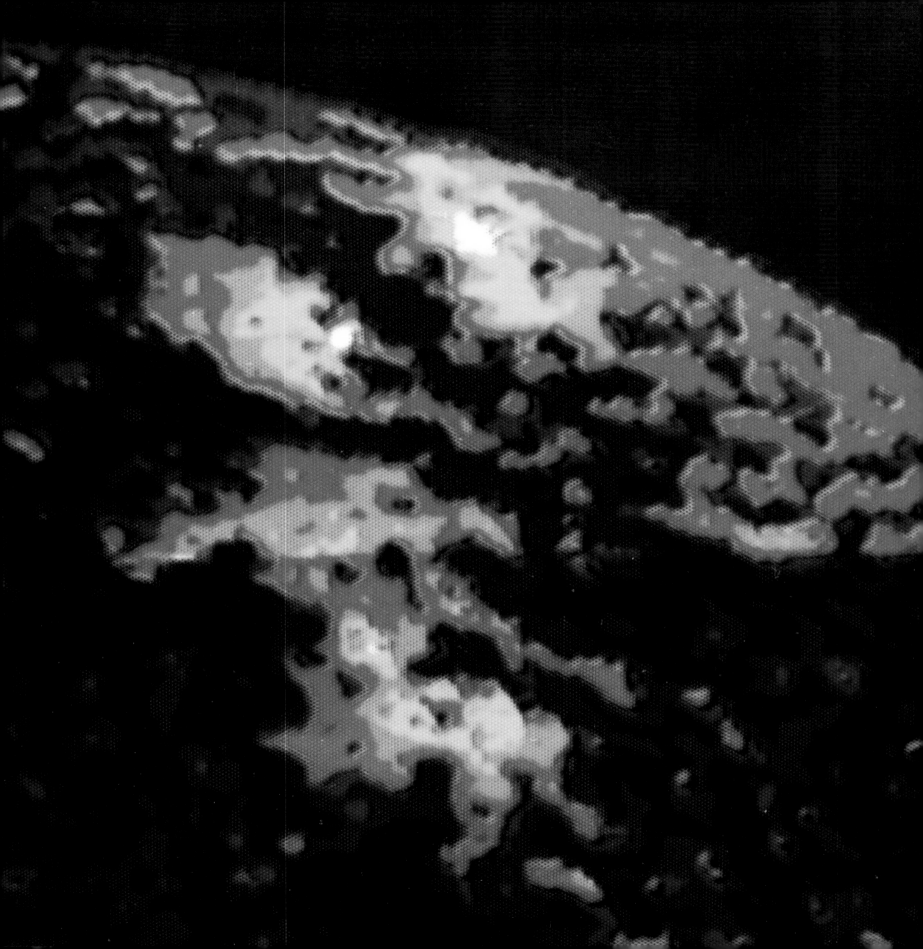

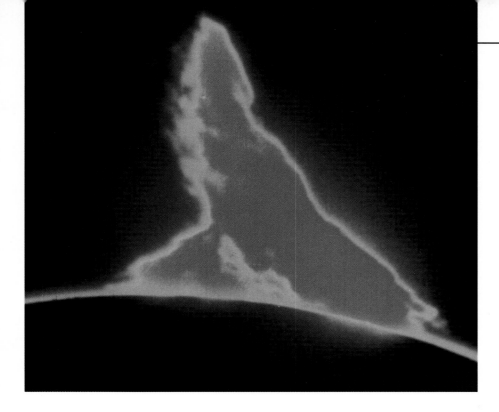

The fury of the Sun manifests itself in numerous ways. On the opposite page, a photograph of the Sun with an ultraviolet-sensitive camera shows variations in temperature near the Sun's surface.

Solar eruptions (left and below) are another sign of the Sun's activity. These emissions send x-ray and radio waves throughout the solar system.

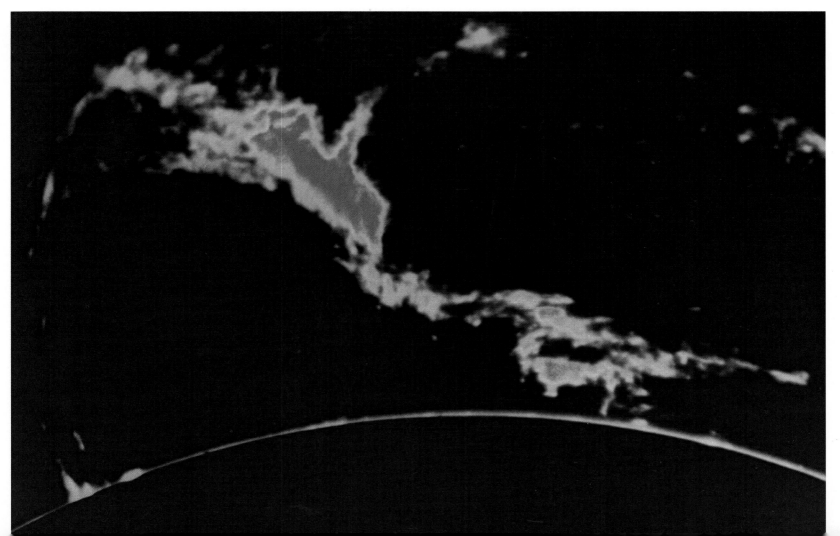

Initially, astronomers could only learn about the Sun's internal processes by watching the progress of sunspots across the Sun's surface. Later, they realized that once solar eclipses could be reliably forecasted, they would be particularly informative occurrences. After hundreds of years of Earth-based observation, scientific inquiry finally had the capacity to extend its examination to the edges of our own planet's domain. Previously, man knew only of the Sun's photosphere, the opaque outer layer that hid its inner workings from sight.

In the years before and after World War II, however, astronomers learned much about the Sun from the areas outside the visual range of light. Radio waves, ultraviolet light, X-rays, and a steady stream of charged particles were studied to gain a greater understanding of our star. Radio astronomy was first discovered in 1931 by a physicist for Bell Telephone who realized that some of the static creeping into radio broadcasts was actually coming to Earth from outer space. This science advanced quickly, and by the 1950s proved particularly useful for studying such solar activities as flares and sunspots (a darkened region on the Sun's surface that features lower temperatures and a greater magnetic field). Ground-based, it focused on a portion of the large radio waves able to pass through the very atmosphere that screens out other wavelengths. Radio astronomy has proved incredibly useful in planetary exploration, as will be seen in future chapters, as well as interstellar and intergalactic study.

In 1946, a U.S. Navy V-2 rocket photographed a portion of the Sun's ultraviolet spectrum from a height of fifty miles, still within the outer layers of the earth's atmosphere, but freed from

The science of radio astronomy helped usher in a new generation of inquiry. Enormous dish antennae point skyward to receive information from and about the Sun and the planets.

In the future, the Hubbell Space Tele-scope will allow astronomers to view objects in and beyond our solar system without the interference of Earth's ob-fuscating atmosphere. This artist's ren-dering shows what the orbiting scope will look like once it has been de-ployed.

much of the interference that protects the surface from those hazardous rays. Unmanned and suborbital, the mission was a quiet step into the era of space-based astronomy. Since then, both manned and unmanned missions sponsored by numerous countries have far exceeded those early observations, but the concept remains the same. The development of America's Hubbell Space Telescope is only the most conspicuous example of our continuing struggle to transcend the earth's meddlesome atmosphere, which makes possible our existence while obscuring our view.

X-ray astronomy also began in the 1940s, though it only reached fruition a few decades later. The Skylab missions of the early 1970s marked the culmination of advancements made in the development of high-quality X-ray images, but this takes us ahead of ourselves in our chronology of solar exploration. It is impossible to consider man's understanding of the Sun without remembering the groundbreaking voyages of the first orbital satellites.

In recent years, much has been made of the political, educational, and social effects of the early space race upon society. However, few studies of these effects take into account the amazing scientific breakthroughs that resulted from those initial missions. While the earliest orbital satellites were primitive, short-lived intruders into space, they did provide theorists the opportunity for direct observations. The early *Sputnik* and *Explorer* launches focused primarily on the earth, circling around the edge of its domain much the same way the planets circle the Sun. The next generation of probes began to explore outward. Between 1958 and 1962 astronomers

The solar corona as seen through one of Skylab's eight telescopes. Color coded to distinguish the levels of brightness, this photograph illustrates how far the Sun reaches out into space. The solar surface is the dark ball at the center, since its brilliance would wash out the fragile light of the corona.

rediscovered the solar system. On its way to take the first photos of the Moon's far side in 1959, the Soviet *Luna 3* recorded the first direct measurements of the solar wind. Those measurements showed astronomers only a wispy remnant of the previously mentioned T Tauri winds (page 15), but provided information from which they could now discern a great deal about the Sun. One chronicler of space exploration stated, ''The discovery of the solar wind by the first interplanetary spacecrafts is among the most important revelations of the entire space program.''

In 1962, the United States launched the *Mariner 2* to further investigate the Soviet's discovery. It found a solar wind, consisting mostly of protons and electrons, that streamed as far out into the solar system as could be measured. In subsequent years, man's most sophisticated probes—including those traveling to the very outskirts of the solar system—have yet to reach a point where the Sun's wind is not detectable. Wherever that point may be, it can be seen as the boundary between the solar domain and interstellar space. As we have learned, however, such a boundary is sure to be vague.

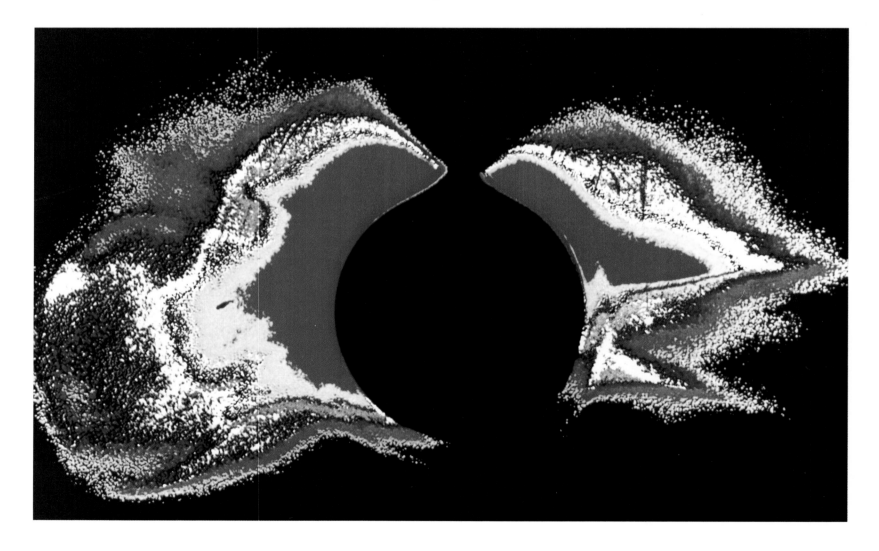

Every manned and unmanned mission ever launched has in some way concerned itself with the effects of the Sun. Whether seeking to tap into its radiation in order to power on-board systems, or to study its physical composition, the Sun is the central focus of any examination of the solar system. In the 1970s, the publicly unheralded Skylab missions were launched to study the Sun, among other things. Less spectacular than the lunar landings, these Skylab missions offered an excellent opportunity for the scientific community to take a closer look at the Sun.

Looking for the source of the solar wind, the Skylab missions focused on the corona. Ultraviolet and X-ray imaging suggested that the corona is not comprised of flames licking out into space, but rather of loops of gas connecting separate points on the solar surface. The corona could be described as the sun's atmosphere, though it is incredibly more rarified than our own. In fact, the density of matter in the Sun's corona is comparable to that of an artificially created vacuum in a laboratory here on Earth. It registers a temperature of 2,000,000 K (considerably higher than the Sun's surface), but it is so rarified that its effect on interplanetary space is negligible.

Even the earliest students of solar eclipses realized that the corona offers important information about the inner layers of the sun. Its dazzling light show provides scientists with the opportunity to study the effects of internal activity. From our knowledge of the corona and more direct studies of the solar surface and the chromosphere (the thin layer connecting the corona and the solar surface), we have come closer to understanding what takes place within our nearest star.

The most recent breakthroughs in solar exploration were brought about by the Space Shuttle-launched Spacelab projects. In December of 1983, the Space Shuttle *Columbia* carried *Spacelab 1* into orbit. The module had been built by the European Space Agency, and with it came the first European to fly aboard a U.S. craft. *Spacelab 2* was aboard the last American shuttle mission before the *Challenger* tragedy.

In 1985, *Spacelab 2*'s photographs of solar granulation provided scientists the best view yet of the Sun's surface. It confirmed their suspicions that the surface oscillates for periods of minutes and hours. These fluctuations allow it to first absorb the radiation emerging from below, and then spew it out through the corona. Despite these informative clues, the complex interaction of sun spots, solar flares, and other forms of solar activity has yet to be completely resolved. Current theory shows an internal dynamo (a device that uses motion within a magnetic field to create energy) carrying the Sun's internal energy out through the radiative zone to eventually be released from the surface. In the same way geologists study waves passing through the earth's crust to learn more about its interior, solar seismology has been developed to learn more about the Sun's inner workings.

While it takes the solar wind merely five days to reach Earth, it is believed that internal radiation takes as much as ten million years to work its way from the Sun's core to its surface. Recent experiments have tried to bypass this interference by searching for neutrinos. These are highly excited particles able to pass through most objects at the speed of light. As a result, they emerge unimpeded from the Sun's internal reactor in a remarkable 2.3 seconds. While being able to measure these neutrinos would provide scientists with first hand information about the Sun's internal workings, their very nature makes it nearly impossible to do so. Since neutrinos pass through objects so easily, they rarely leave any signs of their transit. In the sixties, studies were tentatively begun along these lines, and since then have grown to include huge tanks of chlorine solution buried deep underground in abandoned mines. A certain isotope of chlorine is one of the few elements known to interact with neutrinos, and the liquid's distance from the surface is intended to counteract the effects of other forms of radiation incapable of penetrating the solid objects that neutrinos pass through so easily.

To date, the search for these neutrinos has been inconclusive. In 1986, calculations by Cornell professor Hans Bethe (who played an important role in the making of the atomic bomb) expanded upon a recent Russian hypothesis that may allow more accurate neutrino measurement. Other projects have been started since American scientist Raymond Davis first began his chlorine-based search. These new experiments use liquid argon or heavy water in the hope of capturing the elusive neutrino and learning from it. One project in Kamioka, Japan registered a barrage of neutrinos in connection with the supernova of 1987, lending greater credence to the theory itself.

Meanwhile, a number of other ongoing and future projects are in the works. While the *Voyager* missions have gained their greatest acclaim for exploring the outer planets, they too have studied the effects of the Sun and the solar wind over great distances. (The Very Large Array radio telescope that will play a great role in tracking *Voyager 2* as it flies past Neptune is also being used to gather more information on the Sun.) At this time, the most promising of planned missions is the one created by the European Space Agency, to be launched by a U.S. Space Shuttle around 1990. Both the mission and the probe have been named Ulysses, in honor of the Greek mythological explorer whose journeys took him where no others had traveled.

Ulysses will actually begin its voyage by traveling outwards from the Sun towards Jupiter. Upon reaching that planet, the spacecraft will swing north of the planet's equator before being "snapped" into an orbit that will eventually bring it within two astronomical units (twice the average distance between the Sun and Earth) of the Sun's southern pole. Nine months later, nearly five years after launch, *Ulysses* will make a similar pass over the northern pole.

Until now, *Voyager 1* has attained the highest elevation above the ecliptic plane, reaching a position thirty-five degrees above it. To conjecture what *Ulysses* may find is difficult. All of man's previous explorations have taken place within the ecliptic plane, the area once occupied by the coalescing solar nebula. At what distance above the ecliptic that domain gives way, or undergoes enough change in properties to be considered a separate entity, is uncertain. The vantage point provided by this mission will not only allow scientists to study the flow of energy from the Sun, but perhaps also to detect particles and rays entering our solar system from beyond.

Exactly what we will learn from *Ulysses* remains to be seen, but its ability to provide us with a new vantage point from which to study the Sun is certain to introduce us to new aspects of the Sun's activities. The more we are able to learn, the better we can understand not just our life-giving star, but our planet and those around us. It may seem obvious at this point, but no other object in our small corner of the sky is as important to us as the Sun. By better understanding it we will open the doors to scientific advances here on Earth. Studies of the Sun's magnetic/plasma interaction could teach us safer ways of controlling nuclear-generated energy, while a firmer grasp of the interaction between solar activity and weather here on Earth could also be quite useful.

From the Sun came the planets, possibly nine of them. In different shapes and sizes, pasts and futures, they form a wondrous collection. In the future we may discover other solar systems (astronomers have already detected brown dwarfs, giant planets/failed stars, around nearby stars), and perhaps they too will offer an impressive assortment of planets. But here at the end of the twentieth century, in our own little corner of the sky, we are in the process of discovering our neighboring worlds. Already, they have provided us with breathtaking glimpses of their beauty, while only hinting at all they have to offer.

Eclipses

IT IS A TESTAMENT TO THE SOLAR SYSTEM'S INTRICATE GEOMETRY THAT SOLAR ECLIPSES ARE VISIBLE to us at all. Our Moon just happens to be the perfect size and distance from Earth to play its role in a drama the likes of which takes place nowhere else among the planets. The lunar shadow barely reaches our surface at all, cutting a swath no more than three hundred kilometers across the earth's surface. (In fact, when the Moon is at its greatest distance from Earth, the apogee of its orbit, the shadow from an eclipse would fall short of our surface by more than 30,000 kilometers.) Four hundred times closer than the Sun, yet with a diameter four hundred times smaller, the Moon, at these infrequent times, aligns to block out the entire photosphere. What we are left to behold at these special times are flaming tongues of solar activity licking out into space, the Sun's corona.

Normally the corona is washed out by the overpowering glow of the Sun itself. The photosphere radiates one million times the brightness of the corona, obscuring it from our view. Until recently, astronomers had to wait for the unreliable eclipses to occur, often in remote locales or hindered by poor weather. Fortunately the weather held in 1919, when astronomers claimed to have verified Einstein's General Theory of Relativity. Only during an eclipse could they measure the effects of the Sun's gravitational field on light from distant stars that Einstein had predicted. Proponents of such recent hypotheses as the Superstring Theory continue to question the accuracy of Einstein's theory, but his remains the best known and perhaps the most convincing.

In 1930, a French astronomer named Bernard Lyot, invented the coronagraph, a telescope with photographic capabilities that could simulate an eclipse by artificially blocking out the Sun's photosphere. While the coronagraph may have made solar research easier, it has in no way eclipsed the popularity of the real thing. Solar eclipses are certainly the most photogenic events in our solar system. And yet the most accessible display of the Sun's outward energy is actually an obstructed view. Only by glimpsing the dazzling beauty of its fringes can we even begin to grasp the fury of the Sun's core.

At the point of total eclipse, the corona shines upon the earth with comparable brightness to the full moon. Stars appear in the darkened sky, and the temperature drops. Lasting just a few minutes, the umbra (that part of the shadow in which a total eclipse is visible) cuts a thin path across thousands of miles of the earth's surface. Today we are able to predict such occurrences quite easily, but the earliest spectators must have been very confused. To them the unexpected event was a shocking contradiction of one of the few immutable truths they knew; every day the Sun would rise up on one side of the earth and set down on the other, giving way to night in its time. While the Moon and stars came and went, the Sun was believed to be a constant.

Though many are still caught by surprise during solar eclipses, others travel great distances to be present for them. Both the grant-supported astronomers and the wealthy amateurs turn out, from Nova Scotia to Indonesia. Few and far between, total solar eclipses are once in a lifetime events for most people. Unfortunately, residents of the North American continent will not see another one before the year 2017.

PART II

The TERRESTRIAL PLANETS

ONCE ASTRONOMERS UNDERSTOOD THE NATURE OF THE INDIVIDUAL PLANETS THEY DIVIDED them into two clearly defined categories. The four closest to the Sun are known as the Terrestrial Planets, all orbiting within the asteroid belt that occupies space between Mars and Jupiter. To the other side of this convenient boundary, all the outer planets with the exception of poor Pluto share characteristics that have caused them to be known as the Gas Giants.

For the sake of continuity, our study of the planets will adhere to these classifications. In this section we will examine those Terrestrial brethren—Mercury, Venus, Earth, and Mars—whose creation and geologic growth followed fairly similar patterns. Though their present circumstances run the gamut of possible atmospheres and temperatures, they have more in common than one might initially imagine.

During the formation of the solar system, the Terrestrial Planets began as small planetesimals, solid grains of interstellar dust clumped together. Swirling through the primordial solar nebula, they collided again and again with similar rocky objects. Through these collisions they grew larger, developing a greater gravitational force in the process. The proto-planets grew quickly (perhaps exponentially) as a result. When enough matter had come together, the pressure at the center of these proto-planets raised the temperature to a point where solid turned to liquid. In each of these inner planets a process called differentiation took place, where the heaviest molten material sank towards the center, pushing lighter elements towards the surface. This explains the presence of iron at the core of all the Terrestrials, and even our Moon.

Some time around four-and-a-half billion years ago, the Terrestrial Planets cooled enough to form solid crusts. Some of those surfaces have withstood aeons of meteoric assault, while others have undergone changes within the turmoil of their own atmospheres. They are composed of much of the same stellar dust, and all share remarkably similar mean densities, particularly when compared to those of the Gas Giants.

We'll examine the Terrestrial Planets one at a time, working our way out through the small cluster of worlds circling closely around the Sun. Each tells a different tale of planetary evolution. Each offers a story all its own, a separate clue to the puzzle of solar history.

Mars

The Earth

The Moon

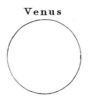

Venus

Mercury

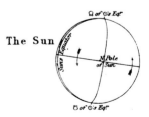

The Sun

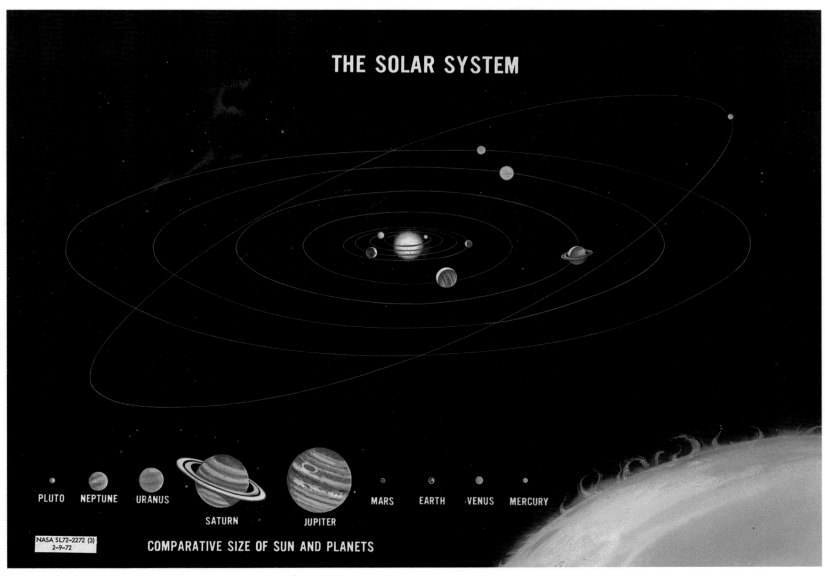

THE SOLAR SYSTEM

PLUTO NEPTUNE URANUS

SATURN

JUPITER

MARS EARTH VENUS MERCURY

NASA SL72-2272 (3)
2-9-72

COMPARATIVE SIZE OF SUN AND PLANETS

By the eighteenth century, astronomers had established a fairly accurate understanding of planetary dimensions (left). Today, however, our models are a bit more precise (above). The smaller Terrestrial Planets can be seen traveling close to the Sun when compared to the vast orbits of the outer Gas Giants.

MERCURY

FROM OUR VANTAGE ON EARTH, MERCURY HAS ALWAYS BEEN A HAZY, FLEETING VISITOR. ITS proximity to the Sun, and rapid orbit around it, are such that the tiny planet is only visible at dusk and dawn, when viewing conditions are least favorable. Its appearances last just a few days at a time, occurring sporadically throughout the earth year. Ancient civilizations believed Mercury to be two different planets and had a name for each, while early twentieth century astronomers drew maps of its "fixed dark side" until discovering that such did not exist. Until recently, very little was known about the innermost planet.

It doesn't say much for Mercury's status among the planets that it is most often compared to our Moon, only a satellite. In size and appearance, the two are quite similar. Both are littered

with craters that are billions of years old, and both have remained essentially unchanged. Neither possesses any real atmosphere, nor gives any indication of substantial internal activity. They spin quietly through space, dead testaments to the earliest stages of planetary development.

As it happens, Mercury's orbit around the Sun is one of the most irregular in the solar system. Its long elliptic path is more exaggerated than any planet but Pluto's, and its deviation from the ecliptic plane ranks second to that wasteland. Mercury swings within 46 million kilometers of the Sun at its closest point in orbit and nearly 70 million kilometers away at its farthest point. (In comparison, the earth never moves more than four percent from a circular orbit.)

Mercury orbits around the sun in a complicated rosette pattern that perplexed astronomers and physicists for a long time. During the nineteenth century, astronomers tracking the orbit of recently discovered Uranus came to believe that a farther planet was responsible for the

Mercury's surface stands as a testament to the ravages of time. Sailing unprotected and close to the Sun, it has spent the last four billion years being battered by large and small particles. This view of the planet was provided by the Mariner 10 spacecraft in 1974 during the last Mercury mission.

eccentricities in its orbit. Employing the same logic that had led them to the discovery of Neptune, they looked for a similar explanation of Mercury's elliptic irregularities. Urbain Leverrier, a French astronomer, correctly predicted Neptune's position in the sky. Soon thereafter he put forth the idea that a small planet even closer to the Sun was responsible for the otherwise inexplicable nature of Mercury's orbit.

Proponents of this theory were so confident of the planet's existence that they christened it Vulcan after the Roman god of fire. A search was begun for the hypothetical world, and in 1859 an unknown amateur claimed to have tracked Vulcan in transit across the Sun. Leverrier was convinced of the amateur's success and celebrated his newest discovery, but others were increasingly skeptical. A total eclipse in 1878 provided the perfect opportunity to confirm Vulcan's existence, but proved fruitless. By the turn of the century astronomers no longer believed in the Frenchman's Vulcan, but they were no closer to explaining Mercury's orbit.

We jump to 1915 and a new set of physical laws being formulated by Albert Einstein. His General Theory of Relativity was actually a theory of gravitation, introducing the idea that enormous gravitational forces could warp time and bend light. According to these laws, Mercury's orbit would accelerate as it came closer to the Sun and slow down as it moved farther away. While each revolution around the Sun took eighty-eight days, Mercury's progress was not fluid. Instead, according to Einstein, it lurched and lagged during the extremes of its eccentric orbit, creating a pattern that defied standard Newtonian gravitational theory.

An interesting result of this complex orbit is that at perihelion, the point at which it is closest to the sun, Mercury rotates on its axis more slowly than it moves in its orbit. Since its day and year are normally quite close in duration, this change creates a situation where it is traveling around the Sun quicker than it is spinning. For the equivalent of a few Earth days, a person standing on Mercury's surface would see the Sun stop in its path across the sky and actually move backwards to the east. Once the planet begins to distance itself from the Sun its speed decreases, and the Sun resumes its normal westward migration against Mercury's airless black sky. Observers at certain points on the Mercurian surface would actually see the Sun rise in the east, return back below the horizon, and then emerge again a few hours later. (The solar eclipse of 1919 further confirmed Einstein's theory, cementing the validity of his explanation for Mercury's orbital irregularities.) To further enhance this remarkable display, from Mercury the Sun appears twice as large at perihelion as at aphelion (that point in an objects orbit at which it is farthest from the Sun), emphasizing the already fascinating anomalies in Mercury's orbit.

Almost everything we now know about Mercury has been learned in the past few decades. In 1965, radio astronomers decided to check the long-standing belief that Mercury always kept one side facing the Sun, in the same way the Moon orbits the earth. By bouncing radio waves off of Mercury's surface, scientists at the Arecibo radio telescope in Puerto Rico discovered that the Mercurian day was not equal to its eighty-eight-day year. Instead they measured its sidereal rotation (the amount of time it takes for an object to revolve once, as measured against a fixed

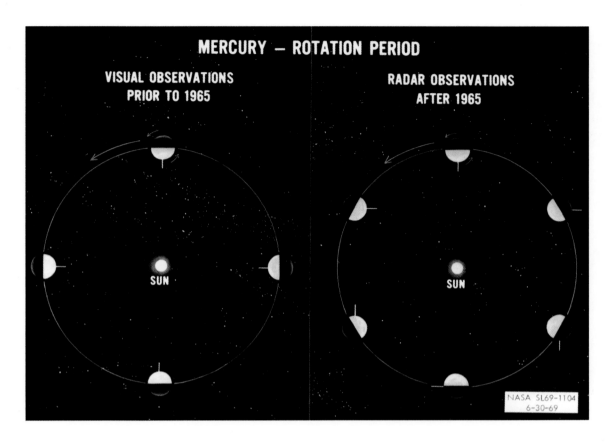

MERCURY — ROTATION PERIOD

VISUAL OBSERVATIONS
PRIOR TO 1965

RADAR OBSERVATIONS
AFTER 1965

SUN

SUN

NASA SL69-1104
6-30-69

Astronomers realized only recently that Mercury's periods of rotation and revolution differ from original calculations. This diagram shows how early theorists imagined Mercury's orbit (left), and what we now understand it to be.

background) to be fifty-nine days, or exactly two thirds the length of its year. This precise resonance means that a complete day, from sunrise to sunrise takes two Mercurian years. (The math gets a bit complicated here, so interested readers might enjoy looking into the various measurements used in calculating planetary movement, including sidereal and synodic rotations, solar rotation periods, etc.)

It is believed that Mercury once spun considerably faster than it does presently, but that it fell prey to the incredible attraction of the nearby Sun. A process known as gravitational interlock is believed to have been at work, slowing the planet down by "grabbing hold" of a bulge in the Mercurian surface. Similar forces are believed to be responsible for the Moon's orbit about Earth, though it remains uncertain whether the Sun's steady force may eventually pull Mercury into the pattern scientists had once believed it to follow.

Further ground-based studies were conducted on Mercury, but the majority of our present knowledge was provided by the *Mariner 10* mission. Launched in 1973, the probe took a look at Venus before encountering Mercury in March of 1974, in the first mission to visit two different planets. Passing within seven hundred kilometers of Mercury's pockmarked surface, *Mariner* would eventually photograph more than half the planet's features. It revealed the Moonlike terrain we now know and introduced us to the remnants of one of the most cataclysmic events in planetary history: The Caloris Basin.

The Caloris Basin is actually a fairly normal crater in some ways, but its extraordinary size (relative to the size of the planet it resides upon) distinguishes it from all others in our solar system. The Basin, 1,300 kilometers in width, is more than a quarter of the width of the planet itself. Caused by an impact of unimaginable force, fallout from the Caloris blast can be found throughout all the rest of Mercury's surface, and some believe the blast is also responsible for periods of heavy meteoric activity elsewhere within the inner planets, particularly Earth's Moon. Unfortunately, we have no real geologic time scale for Mercury, so it is hard to confirm or deny this theory. Though the magnitude of the Caloris impact is certainly remarkable, it makes sense that it would have occurred on Mercury. The small planet travels faster through space than the others, and its essentially nonexistent atmosphere would do nothing to diminish the force of the impact. This and its diminutive size make Mercury a leading candidate for a feature such as the Caloris Basin.

A seemingly unrelated section of perplexing features, simply termed Weird Terrain by normally technical scientists, was also discovered in the mapping of the planet, initially stumping astronomers and geologists alike. The rugged, jumbled landscape revealed by *Mariner* was like nothing else seen among the planets, and its cause remained elusive. Eventually, it was realized that the Weird Terrain occurred at the antipodes (opposite) to the Caloris Basin (the point on the planet's surface directly opposite the enormous impact crater). This has led scientists to believe that the impact responsible for Caloris was so great it sent shock waves rippling through the young planet. When those waves met on the far point of the planet's surface they combined to create enormous, chaotic, seismic activity, resulting in the Weird Terrain.

While *Mariner 10* confirmed the existence of some volcanic activity on Mercury's surface, it is believed almost all of this activity was instigated by collisions with external bodies. We now believe that within two hundred million years of its formation, Mercury's outer layer reached its highest temperature, before cooling off into a malleable, plasticized surface. As the core cooled, so did the surface; since that time impact accounts for nearly all changes.

Perhaps the most surprising find of the *Mariner 10* mission, however, was its discovery of Mercury's weak magnetic field. Spinning as slowly upon its axis as it does, Mercury was not expected to possess any magnetic field at all. We now believe the field exists because of a disproportionately large iron core at the planet's center. Thought to be responsible for as much as three-quarters of the entire size of the planet, Mercury's core is greater than that of any of the other Terrestrial Planets. The fledgling planet's proximity to the Sun stripped it of the lighter elements that could have led to a mass more like that of Venus or Earth. It lost most of these light elements to the massive star's enormous gravitational pull; the remainder blew off into space as Mercury stood full in the face of the tremendous T Tauri winds discussed in relation to the Sun's formation.

The discovery of Mercury's substantial iron core has also proved helpful in explaining a recurring Mercurian surface feature: scarps. These are long lines of cliffs running hundreds of

NASA's Venus-Mercury swingby was an early attempt to use one mission to study more than one planet. This successful endeavor gave scientists a better understanding of the subjects listed in this artist's rendering (opposite page).

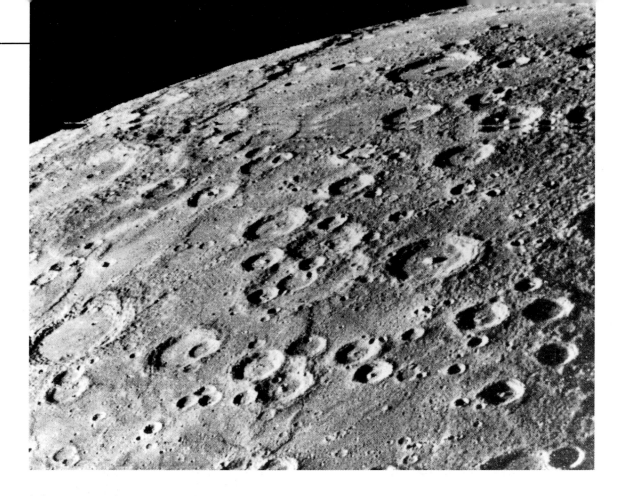

A scarp cuts across Mercury's surface, seen in the center of this photograph and running south. It runs across and around impact craters, nearly six hundred kilometers in length. This photograph was taken by Mariner 10 less than 80,000 kilometers from the planet's surface.

kilometers in length, unrelated to any other nearby geologic activity. Today we believe these scarps came about as the planet's core began to cool. It shrank, eroding support from the crust which wrinkled to keep pace. While tectonic plates on Earth were able to shift and accommodate these changes, Mercury's unyielding surface puckered instead.

Shortly after completing its first pass of the small barren planet, *Mariner 10* was reprogrammed to enter into an orbit around the Sun that would allow it to continue passing Mercury each time around. Two subsequent encounters were possible before the craft's directional equipment gave out. *Mariner 10* continues to circle the Sun, deaf to our communications and incapable of transmitting further data. In its three passes, however, the probe provided us with many years worth of data. Only in this decade have we finally digested this information to formulate our current picture of Mercury.

One major surprise found in this growing picture was the discovery, in 1985, of sodium in Mercury's thin atmosphere. Researchers at the University of Texas came across its presence while studying spectral lines in visible light. (Unfortunately *Mariner 10* had been conducting such searches only in the ultraviolet range and missed detecting this.) Mercury's ultra-thin atmosphere is insufficient to retain the sodium emitted from the surface, so that source is considered to be steady. Current theory posits that the sodium formed via the planet's interaction with small meteorites and the pervasive solar wind and then floated off into interplanetary space.

A few years ago we were completely unaware of Mercury's sodium emissions. Today we believe that sodium is the most prevalent element in the Mercurian atmosphere. To state anything with great certainty about Mercury, however, can be dangerous. As in past centuries, today's "experts" continue to find themselves fooled by the mysterious planet. Ever the elusive messenger, Mercury brings us tales of the solar system's past before spinning quickly away. At this time, however, there are no missions planned to the barren world hurtling through the solar system in the glare of the Sun. As one mission summary of the planet concluded, *"Mariner 10* has shown us what we wanted to see, and we are in no hurry to return." Recent conferences have shown that many scientists still keep an Earth-based eye trained on tiny Mercury, but the general public remains unenthused about the Moonlike little rock when confronted with the more colorful worlds seen in recent expeditions.

Galileo Galilei, 1564–1642, quickly trained the new telescope on mysterious Venus. His interpretation of the planet's phases led to a greater understanding of the solar system itself. The planet's swirling atmosphere is seen (facing page) through the lens of Mariner 10 on its way to Mercury.

VENUS

SIMILAR IN SIZE, MASS, AND DENSITY TO EARTH, VENUS HAS LONG BEEN KNOWN AS OUR SISTER planet. But when we consider the emphasis the Russian space program has placed upon the cloud-covered world, it might be more appropriate to think of it as our comrade planet. Since 1961, the U.S.S.R. has aimed more than a dozen Venera probes at it, meeting with both great success and great failure. Information from these and numerous American missions have forced us to drastically reevaluate our view of the shrouded planet, a complex world from which we may be able to learn a great deal about our own.

Like Mercury, Venus' position within Earth's orbit has made it difficult to observe. It, too, was believed to have been two distinct planets, one visiting occasionally in the earliest darkness, the other appearing briefly before dawn. Rising first and shining the most brightly, Venus' white disc is often the first light in the darkening sky. ("Star light, star bright, first star I see tonight," is often, in fact, a planet!) Since it was so much closer and larger than Mercury, astronomers were able to see Moonlike phases in Venus' orbit with the earliest telescopes. Galileo sketched its crescent phases over three hundred fifty years ago and understood that phenomenon to confirm that the Sun was indeed the center of the "universe." (Only if Venus were orbiting the Sun would such phases be visible on Earth.)

Venus' brilliance in our sky is exceeded only by the Sun and the Moon and is actually capable of casting shadows on clear, dark nights. Named for the goddess of love, Venus, daughter of Uranus, earned its romantic appellation by shining brightly while remaining shrouded in mystery. Its high albedo (a measure of an object's reflective properties) and thick clouds obscured our view of the surface until the first probes returned photos from the planet during the late 1970s. Before that time, astronomers were left to examine Venus' other properties, drawing on them to create a mental picture of what might be.

In the same way that Galileo's discovery of Venus' phases led him to a greater understanding of the solar system, eighteenth century scientists showed similar ingenuity. Calculations indicated that Venus would transit the Sun twice in succession, in 1763 and 1769. In this case, a transit means that a planet crosses between Earth and the Sun and is visible against that star's enormous surface. Only Mercury and Venus can be seen to do this from our planet. The rapidly orbiting Mercury transits often, every ten years or so. (Next transit: 1999) Venus, however, is a much rarer participant, following yet another of our solar system's complicated patterns. Its transits occur twice over an average of eight years, repeating at intervals of 113 and 130 years. This means that since the transit of 1769, only one other pair has been visible, just before the turn of this century. The next couple will arrive in 2004 and 2012.

Such future transits are more likely to be considered as pleasant rarities, to be savored by the curious, rather than as the informative events they once were. Back before the transits in the 1760s, astronomers were able to calculate the scale of the known solar system but not its size. If

Venus' thick atmosphere made it impossible for early observers to penetrate its mysterious shroud. This photograph, taken by the Pioneer Venus orbiter in 1979, dramatically illustrates how difficult it is for normal visual observations to provide information about what lies below.

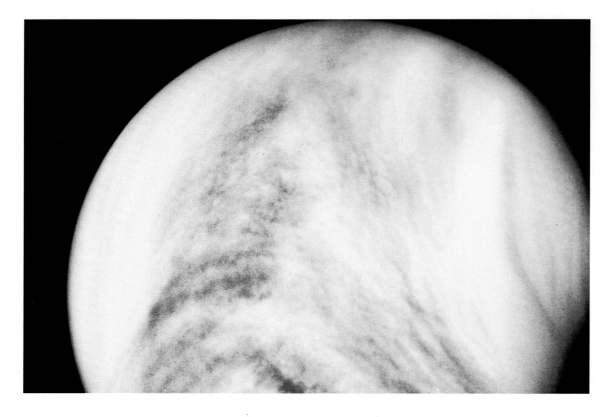

they could determine one measurement, the rest could be deduced from it. In 1769, explorers were dispatched across the globe to measure Venus' transit from as many different perspectives as possible. Compiling the results and computing the angles across millions of miles of space involved some tricky math based on slightly hazy observations, but the results came respectably close to current measurements. Elusive Venus had shed light elsewhere, while giving away none of its own secrets.

The difficulty of obtaining clear views during the transits led a Russian astronomer, Mikhail Lomonsov, to suggest that a turbulent Venusian atmosphere could be responsible for the imprecise readings. A consensus developed that those were clouds all right, perhaps a bit thicker than our own. Thick enough, at least, that we hadn't the slightest idea what lay beneath them. As a result, astronomers put forward a number of interesting proposals, which, in retrospect, ran the gamut from the innocently erroneous to the patently absurd. Nineteenth century scenarios included ritualistic fires celebrating ascendancies to the throne and the existence of a primeval forest similar to those that occurred on Earth during the Carboniferous period some three hundred million years ago.

Well into the twentieth century there was no real basis for even guessing what might lie beneath Venus' veil. The first clues arrived via the fledgling science of radio astronomy. In the 1950s, readings that described Venus as scorchingly hot were dismissed by some as a technical malfunction. In the 1960s astronomers were in for a much greater shock. Bouncing radio waves

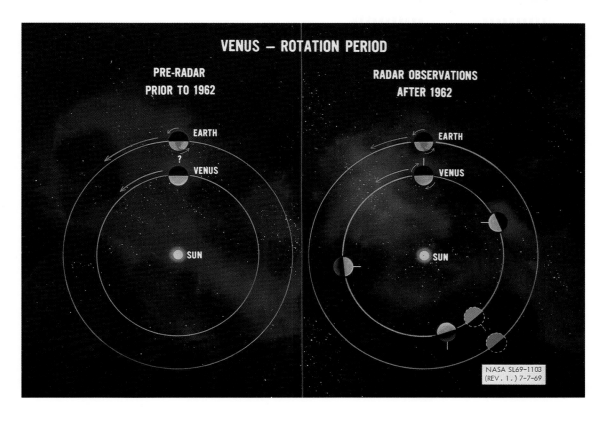

VENUS – ROTATION PERIOD

PRE-RADAR
PRIOR TO 1962

EARTH
?
VENUS
SUN

RADAR OBSERVATIONS
AFTER 1962

EARTH
VENUS
SUN

NASA SL69-1103
(REV. 1.) 7-7-69

Prior to the application of radio astronomy, scientists knew nothing of Venus' rotation. What they discovered—that the planet moved in a retrograde motion—confounded all of the experts. We still can't completely explain the planet's "backwards" rotation, but we at least have been able to measure it.

off Mercury to determine its rotation had destroyed one myth, but this was outdone by the startling result of Venus' test. The planet, they learned, rotated backwards! Scientists remain unable to explain Venus' retrograde motion. They mention large collisions or the formation of a rogue eddy, swirling opposite from its fellow proto-planets, but will quickly admit that they really don't know for sure. Glossed over in most discussions of the planet, Venus' retrograde anomaly remains one of the great unsolved mysteries in our solar system.

Combined sources were beginning to paint a picture of a super-heated landscape buffeted by tremendous winds of carbon dioxide driven by clouds of sulfuric acid. (Perhaps it's no coincidence that sci-fi propagators of the 1950s and 1960s quickly made Mars the futuristic battleground of choice.) The U.S. *Mariner 2* mission passed Venus in December, 1962—the first man-made probe to reach another planet. After having trouble with the first three Venera probes dating back to 1961, the Russians successfully launched *Venera 4* in June of 1967. This probe ejected a capsule into the Venusian atmosphere, which transmitted information for more than an hour before giving out. The next two Venera probes also succumbed before reaching the planet's surface, by which time it was fairly well established that great atmospheric pressure was literally crushing the capsules out of existence.

We now know that the pressure at the surface of Venus is equal to the pressure on Earth, one thousand meters below sea level. In addition, temperatures were confirmed to go as high as 750K. This seems remarkably high when one considers that the planet receives enough solar

Topographic maps of Venus (below) and Earth (right) illustrate the similarities and differences between the two planets' surfaces. Two "continents" stand out on the Venusian surface, on Ishtar, the larger one, is the highest point on the planet's surface. The smaller, Aphrodite (seen in the lower right portion of this map) is comparable in scale to Africa.

radiation to account for only half that much heat. Further study eventually created a picture of an atmosphere run amok, trapping incoming heat like a greenhouse does on Earth. The hotter the planet's surface became, the easier it was to retain that heat. In their earliest states, Venus' and Earth's atmospheres may not have been all that different. On the earth, however, temperatures were low enough that carbon dioxide was trapped in rocks and the oceans, creating an atmosphere of nitrogen and free oxygen. That oxygen created an ozone layer that would filter out much of the Sun's radiation.

Meanwhile, Venus' carbon was forming the majority of the planet's atmosphere in the form of carbon dioxide. This raised temperatures, evaporating any water that may have once existed and creating a thick cloud cover that prevented the Sun's heat from escaping. Today scientists are paying particularly close attention to the causes that led to the runaway greenhouse effect on Venus in an attempt to answer growing concerns about the earth's ozone layer and what its destruction could mean to us. In Venus we are confronted with how precarious our own little niche is on Earth and how vulnerable we really are to forces within and beyond our control.

The study of Venus attained new heights in October 1975, when the Soviets landed two experiment-packed probes on the planet's surface. *Venera 9* and *10* sent back the first photos of

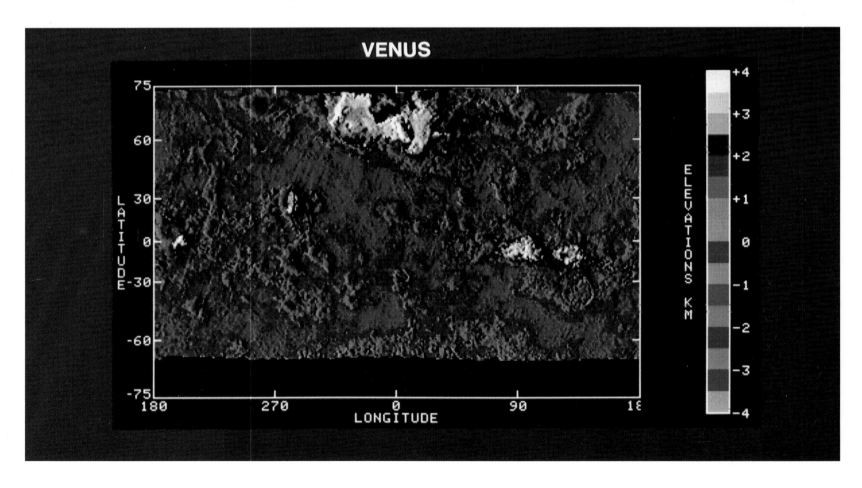

the Venusian surface, and again scientists were surprised. Early measurements of Venus' high-altitude clouds indicated wind speeds sixty times the rate of the planet's rotation, causing most scientists to predict a wind-blown planet of flat, smooth surfaces and whirling dust storms. Both probes brought their own lighting in expectation of the darkness such storm clouds would create.

Instead, *Venera 9* and *10* returned pictures taken in the Sun's natural light, a diffuse glow similar in intensity to an overcast fall day in Moscow. In addition, the photos showed sharp, angular rocks strewn across the surface. Instead of hurricane forces, the *Venera*s actually found soft breezes clocking in at two kilometers per hour. Once again the hard evidence made it necessary to reevaluate our perceptions of the mysterious planet. In 1982, *Venera 13* and *14* sent back color photos before capitulating to the incredible pressures, while the next pair of probes orbited the planet to transmit high-resolution radar maps of the planet's surface. (Experiments based on data collected by the *Venera 13* and *14* probes led a team of Soviet and U.S. researchers to announce in 1986 that photographs from the surface of Venus showed that the black rocks found in the area proved that Venus' oxygen was indeed trapped in its surface.)

Mapping of Venus' surface was started in the 1960s at Arecibo, Puerto Rico, soon after the completion of the experiments that discovered its retrograde motion. The U.S. *Pioneer-Venus 1*

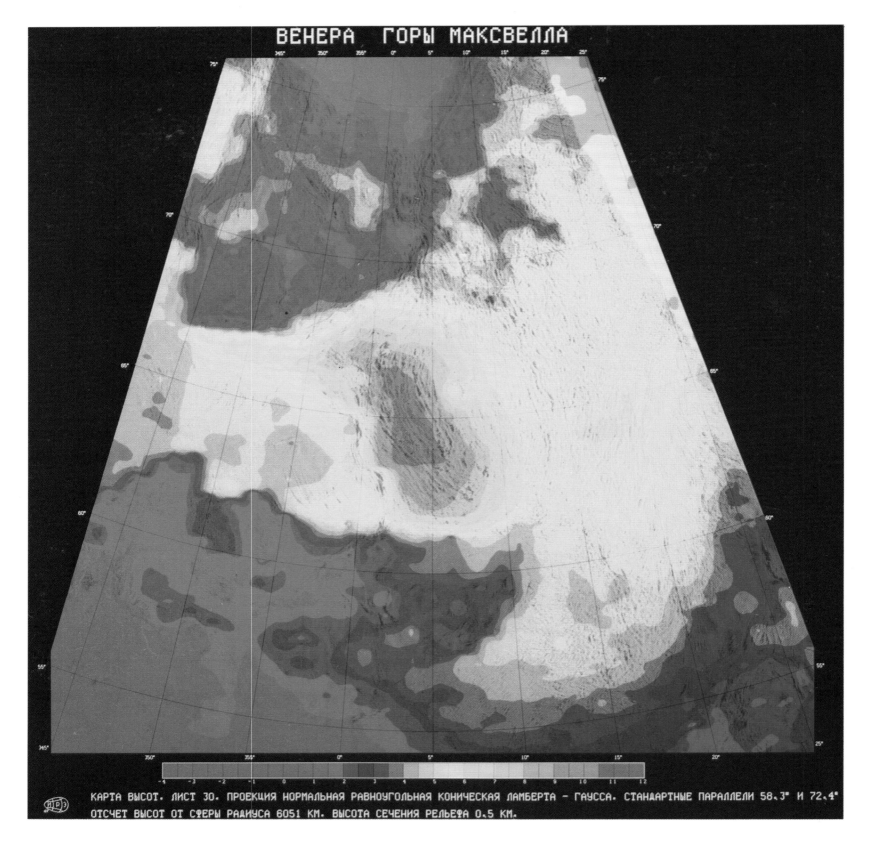

ВЕНЕРА ГОРЫ МАКСВЕЛЛА

КАРТА ВЫСОТ. ЛИСТ 30. ПРОЕКЦИЯ НОРМАЛЬНАЯ РАВНОУГОЛЬНАЯ КОНИЧЕСКАЯ ЛАМБЕРТА - ГАУССА. СТАНДАРТНЫЕ ПАРАЛЛЕЛИ 58,3° И 72,4°
ОТСЧЕТ ВЫСОТ ОТ СФЕРЫ РАДИУСА 6051 КМ. ВЫСОТА СЕЧЕНИЯ РЕЛЬЕФА 0,5 КМ.

mission (*P-V1*) engaged in a great deal of more precise radar mapping in 1980, fleshing out a contour map that presents a variety of continent-like plateaus without an ocean to surround them. The topography of the major plateaus revealed an active geologic past and suggested the possibility of continued activity. In addition to detecting a small elevated feature believed to be a pair of volcanoes, named Beta Regio, the *Pioneer-Venus* orbiter also found shifts in the abundance of sulfur dioxide in the planet's atmosphere, perhaps indicating activity that had taken place just before its arrival. Upon its encounter with the planet, the probe found drastically increased amounts of the gas in the planet's upper atmosphere and continued to monitor its steady decline.

In 1983, *Venera 15* and *16* improved the twenty-kilometer resolution of the *P-V1* with a new imaging system that allowed features as small as one kilometer to be registered. At the time, Western scientists were surprised by the Soviet's development of a synthetic-aperture radar that combined separate readings to achieve a resolution unattainable by current Earth-based systems. But the state of the art changes rapidly in these technological times, and NASA's *Magellan* spacecraft promises to improve on that two to four times over.

The Soviet fascination with the nearby planet remains so strong that their Halley's Comet probe launched in 1985 swung past the planet to drop off a packet of scientific equipment before rendezvousing with the highly anticipated comet. *Vega,* as the mission was named, combined the resources of the Russians and the French, while the portion that continued to Halley's contained experiments provided by a number of nations, the U.S. included. Deploying both a lander and an atmospheric balloon into the Venusian atmosphere, the Vega mission was able to find further evidence of volcanic activity—including lightning caused by the hot gasses released into the atmosphere—and more information about wind currents above the surface.

The Magellan mission, mentioned in regard to its radar capabilities, will also seek to increase our knowledge of Venus' geologic history. It is expected to confirm our belief in a one-plate surface on the planet (unlike Earth's multiple, tectonic plates), while smoothing out the rough edges of our current topographic maps. Unfortunately, though, Venus' crushing pressure and trapped heat seem to have dampened much enthusiasm for extensive surface study. As the Soviet Union indicates an increased interest in studying Mars, and the United States' next potential visit is an atmospheric probe to be launched in the late 1990s, it seems likely that further breakthroughs will be derived from Earth-based studies and the digestion of recently received data.

The Venus of our forefathers, a mysteriously alluring beauty, has been greatly reconsidered in this century. We are left with an equally fascinating but far less inviting world that can tell us a great deal about our own planet. The notion of manned expeditions to Venus remains a vague one at this time, conjuring images of small submarines on wheels, protecting earthlings from the crushing conditions on Venus' inhospitable surface. Yet the many probes, both Russian and American, have proved tremendously helpful in understanding our comrade planet. The picture we have today is far from complete, but it is sufficient enough to dissuade us from looking more closely for now.

The Soviet Venera 15 *probe improved the resolution of previous mappings, and also represented an improvement in cooperation among the superpowers. This image (facing page) from that 1983 mission was presented to NASA a few years later, and subsequent missions have been made available to scientists from many nations.*

EARTH

WHAT'S ALL THIS FUSS ABOUT EARTH? IT IS, AFTER ALL, JUST A SECOND RATE ROCK EXISTING ALONG the fringes of an unexceptional star. It pales in comparison with the enormous Gas Giants, and its surface features seem bland in light of the tremendous canyons and volcanoes found on its Terrestrial counterparts. It would be easy to say that our planet is an unexceptional little world, unduly elevated in status by its "earthnocentric" inhabitants. Easy, but not really true.

When we attempt to view Earth objectively, if such a thing is truly possible, we realize that it really is a special member of the solar system. Our diminutive planet is a statistical wonder; the right size and proper distance from the Sun to permit an incredibly complex animate community to exist. While mighty Jupiter, alluring Saturn, or oppressive Venus each inspires wonder because of their extremes, none offers a hint of what tiny Earth features in such abundance: life.

As members of that unique existence, we tend to see our presence as the ultimate accomplishment in the long history of the solar system. Whether such statistical improbabilities have come together on planets around other stars is the subject of much discussion, rational and otherwise. The laws of probability tell us that life elsewhere is indeed possible, although not highly likely. But of the planets in our solar system, only Earth offers scientists an opportunity to study life directly. Someday Mars or Venus, Titan or Europa, may offer proof of life—past, present, or future. Until then, however, even the most objective study of the solar system forces us to pay keen attention to Earth.

Dry Facts About a Wet Planet

Our intimate familiarity with Earth clouds our ability to perceive it as only one of many planets in this solar neighborhood. Facts and figures used so routinely when discussing other worlds are easily side stepped for the descriptive homages to earthly wonders. Mt. Everest is thought of as a treacherous challenge and the Hawaiian Islands as a great place to vacation. But only when we see them as geological phenomena can we begin to understand them in the context of this planetary examination. The scientific pursuit of comparative planetology—comparing the planets to one another—helps us understand Earth's place in the planetary scheme of things. Such an approach has proved essential to our greater understanding of our neighbors, as well as Earth. Scientists striving to understand the precarious development of life on Earth often turn to nearby worlds for a glimpse at other directions our planet might have taken.

Earth is the third planet from the Sun, orbiting it at an average distance of 149,600,000 kilometers. Its nearest neighbor is Venus, over 40,000 kilometers closer to the Sun, while Mars lies about twice as far from Earth in the other direction. Tiny Mercury, the remaining Terrestrial, is more than half the distance from Earth to the Sun, farther (on average) from our planet than Mars. (While the distances from Earth to the Gas Giants are discussed in future chapters, the

Apollo 17 *captured this image of the African continent and polar cap on its way back from America's last lunar visit. Our planet's colorful presence in the solar system would make it special even without the additional oddity of the life that can be found upon it.*

following illustration may prove helpful: If a scaled-down version of the Sun were placed on the goal line of a football field, Mercury, Venus, and Earth would all sit within the twenty-yard line. Mars would be just inside the thirty, and mighty Jupiter would occupy the opposite goal line, one hundred yards away. Saturn would be another football field away, Uranus four away, and Neptune nearly seven. Pluto, however, would zoom to within six or seven football fields at perigee, before floating back out to a distance ten football fields from the miniature Sun.)

With an equatorial diameter of 12,756 kilometers, Earth is the largest of the Terrestrial planets, a slight fraction wider than its near twin, Venus. It's almost twice the size of Mars, and more than two-and-a-half times that of Mercury. Yet Earth's preeminence among the Terrestrials is quickly rendered moot by comparing it to the enormous outer planets. Uranus and Neptune are each about four times the width of our home planet; Saturn is more than double that, Jupiter nearly triple.

Earth travels around the Sun in a revolution encompassing 365 days. (All planetary revolutions are measured in Earth days, since calculating them in their own days would make any comparison impractical.) During that time, fleet Mercury will have begun its fifth revolution, and Venus would be halfway into its second. Meanwhile, Mars would have completed only half a revolution, and the outer planets just a tiny fraction of their lengthy "years." Jupiter's twelve-year revolution may seem long, but it is negligible when one considers the 165- and 248-year cycles of Neptune and Pluto, respectively.

*Apollo 11 **took the above photograph on its way to the Moon. Though the Apollo missions are duly famous for their lunar focus, they also provided earthlings with superb images of their own planet. This "close-up" (opposite page) was provided by one of NASA's** Landsat **crafts, which orbit Earth taking extremely high resolution photographs of the planet's surface.***

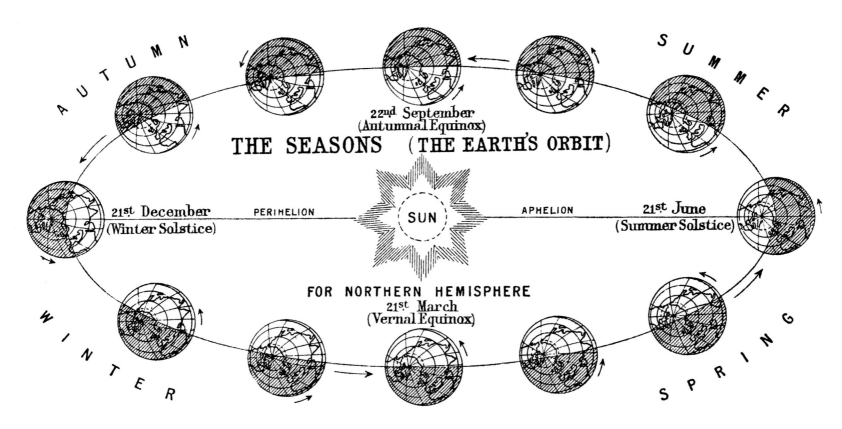

22ⁿᵈ September
(Autumnal Equinox)

THE SEASONS   (THE EARTH'S ORBIT)

21ˢᵗ December
(Winter Solstice)

PERIHELION

SUN

APHELION

21ˢᵗ June
(Summer Solstice)

FOR NORTHERN HEMISPHERE
21ˢᵗ March
(Vernal Equinox)

AUTUMN

SUMMER

WINTER

SPRING

Early on, astronomers realized that Earth's orbit around the Sun was a particularly straightforward one. It deviates very little from a circular orbit— less than any of the other planets.

Along the course of its travels, Earth deviates very little from its orbit; only Venus and Uranus describe less eccentric paths. Earth also stays remarkably close to the ecliptic plane, much more than second place Uranus. In addition, Earth's density is similar to its Terrestrial partners', just slightly higher than that of Mercury and Venus. Physical characteristics—when examined through the impersonal statistics of planetary measurement—do little to distinguish Earth from its lifeless companions. Only when we consider the position of our planet in relation to the Sun, do we begin to see where the differences lie.

Could Venus or Titan have harbored complex life were they farther from, or closer to, the Sun? Was it the composition of the proto-earth that made our existence possible, or simply the ideal, consistent distance from the solar system's principal energy source? A planet that has much in common with its neighbors nonetheless stands out. Earth changes constantly, as do the Gas Giants, while maintaining the firm surface of the Terrestrials. It is the only planet to support life, and it is also considered by some of its inhabitants to be alive itself.

If Earth's orbit were one percent farther from the Sun (a mere million-and-a-half kilometers), all of its water would have frozen some two billion years ago. On the other hand, an orbit five percent closer would have resulted in the vaporization of all liquids, much like Venus. Had young Earth's atmosphere been any thinner, it could not have regulated fluctuations in temperature. If the planet was ten percent larger, too much carbon dioxide would have built up in its atmosphere, and again the results could have been similar to the runaway greenhouse conditions on Venus. A thinner atmosphere or a smaller planetary radius would have prevented the fledgling atmosphere from creating enough ozone to filter out the Sun's deadly ultraviolet rays.

Best of all, young Earth's fortunate circumstances allowed the presence of a particularly useful substance: water—H_2O. And plenty of it. It fell from the skies during the earliest phases of the planet's evolution, once temperatures had sunk below the boiling point. Today, most of the water on Earth is believed to have formed approximately four billion years ago. Its presence provided the ideal medium for life and dissolved most of the earliest atmospheric gasses. The oceans managed to fine-tune an atmosphere that could well have made Earth a twin to Venus in more than just size.

Atmospheric winds traveling at 80 knots are captured in this photo from Apollo 7. Hurricane Gladys raged in 1968, twisting above the Caribbean Sea. This furious storm is part of an intricate system of atmospheric currents and clashes created by the interaction of wind and water.

Running water reshapes the very sur-face of our planet. Proponents of Gaia, who view Earth itself as a living entity, see these changes as a small part of the planet's greater activity.

The word Earth was first used to refer to that upon which we dwelled, the solid, dirt surface below us. Eventually, it changed from meaning soil that could be scooped up by hand to the planet upon which we now stand. In both cases the term had much to do with the user's concept of his or her place in the universe. Current usage rarely refers to the dirt at our feet, but rather to the spinning globe we inhabit. As a planet, Earth represents a number of defined qualities: third planet from the Sun, big fish in the small Terrestrial pond, are only a few of the characteristics which help define Earth. In our minds, however, the big blue marble continues to be viewed through the rose tinted lenses of earthnocentrics. Earth cannot help but receive a great deal of attention in any planetary study, and much of it may actually be appropriate.

Our planet is alive. Not just inhabited, but alive. It is the only Terrestrial whose crust has fundamentally changed, moving since its formation and moving still. Enormous tectonic plates "float" on currents of molten rock, which bubble up from below. The same motion that carried radiation to the Sun's photosphere now brings heat from Earth's core to its surface. That rising heat keeps the large plates grinding into some of their neighbors while pulling away from others. The concept is an old one, first hinted at by many of the ancient legends that tried to explain earthquakes or volcanoes, but finally put forth scientifically in the eighteenth century. In doing so, James Hutton, a leading figure in the age of Scottish Enlightenment, established himself as a founding father of a new science: geology.

The study of geology ushered in science's consideration of our planet as an entity—an object to be studied and understood. The ancients had already determined the size of the sphere they inhabited, but they never completely grasped the implications of the diverse geological features all around them. By the beginning of the twentieth century, however, man's understanding of his surroundings was sharply on the rise. German explorer/scientist Alfred Wegener furthered Hutton's ideas and first coined the term *Pangea* for the primal landmass that eventually broke into the known continents.

There were, however, some flaws in the hypotheses of the early theorists, some of which were not corrected until very recently. In the 1950s, rocks were discovered on the ocean floor that were a mere two hundred million years old. If both Hutton and Wegener's ideas were correct, these rocks should have been billions of years old, part of the rigid layer upon which the continents moved about. The discovery of these young rocks meant that their formation was still taking place, and therefore that the plates along the ocean bottom were themselves still separating, permitting the creation of newer crust. The continents, then, were not icebergs floating over lower levels of crust, but rather the highlands of enormous masses (more like glaciers than icebergs) inexorably transforming the surface of the Earth.

In the Bible, the earth appeared on the third day. (Though the length of those days is the subject of much debate.) Until then, the proto-planet was a spinning ball of gas and molten rock. As it condensed, the orb's heat increased while its surface heat decreased. The resulting

The abundance of life on Earth is unparalleled anywhere else in our solar system. Though earthlings may take its variety for granted at times, lush vistas such as this one are testament to the special place our planet occupies.

© Derek Fell

surface-to-volume ratio rendered the sphere incapable of releasing all of the center's energy. The process of differentiation (in which heavier material collects at the center and lighter ones float to the top) separated the heavier elements that would eventually form the planet's iron-nickel core from lighter silicates. Within one hundred million years of its formation, as its crust hardened, Earth had established the basic internal structure that exists today.

That fledgling surface was probably surrounded by a good deal of both hydrogen and helium. Those gasses would be blown away during the course of the Sun's T Tauri assault. Only once that clean sweep had been made did the atmosphere we currently inhabit begin to form. It arrived through Earth's porous new crust as gasses escaped from the planet's internal fury. Volcanoes and meteorites helped create a carbon dioxide atmosphere, parts of which were easily converted into trace amounts of methane and ammonia. The oceans were filled by the remaining hydrogen, able to pull oxygen atoms from their carbon bonds.

Though the earliest stages of the atmosphere's development only slightly resemble present conditions, they were directly responsible for its current composition. One billion years after the planet's formation, the earliest primordial soup was beginning to boil over. Though the development of living cells took billions of years, they eventually managed to recreate the planet's atmosphere. Consuming the available carbon dioxide (CO_2), the most primitive organisms produced oxygen as a waste product. Eventually they consumed so much CO_2 that the atmosphere consisted solely of nitrogen and oxygen. While oxygen gets a great deal of credit for filtering harmful rays and providing a breathable atmosphere, nitrogen still constitutes nearly eighty percent of our atmosphere and is essential for all living tissue.

In other chapters, planetary atmospheres are often given less attention than is Earth's. Considering the direct effect it has on our existence, we earthlings take obvious interest in our atmosphere. It protects us from the hazards of solar radiation and filters the majority of meteoric visitors. (As a result, impact craters are so rare on Earth that they have been turned into national parks and research sites.)

Unfortunately, the more we learn about Earth's atmosphere, the more aware we are of the risks we are taking with it. Irresponsible industry and shortsighted governments have permitted the buying and selling of our skies to the point where the next few hundred years (a quick tick of the planetary clock) could well bring about drastic alterations in the ozone layer. While earthquakes and volcanoes remain beyond our control, the atmosphere is more than literally in our hands.

Continued internal rumblings passing along the edges of Earth's tectonic plates move quite slowly, but they will eventually effect drastic changes in our environment. Some contemporary scientists present the idea that Earth itself is a living organism; not necessarily conscious, but operating along the principles of simple cells maintaining conditions conducive to survival. British scientist James Lovelock introduced this concept as *Gaia,* named for the Greek mythological equivalent of Mother Earth.

If Earth, then, is alive, interesting questions arise about other planets. The idea also makes one wonder about the role the Moon plays in Earth's existence. Our satellite, the only major one to orbit a Terrestrial planet, has had an incalculable effect on the development of Earth. Orbits, tides, eclipses, and illumination are just a few of the Moon's contributions to our existence. Some believe the tides allowed the primordial soup to be properly stirred; others maintain that the expulsion of lunar material was essential to the eventual presence of life.

Earthrise. As the Apollo 11 astronauts rounded the far side of the Moon, they were greeted by this stunning view of home. The lunar surface is rendered particularly bland and monochromatic when contrasted with the swirling colors of the planet around which it revolves.

Extra-terrestrial exploration of Earth began as soon as scientists had developed rockets strong enough to blast experimental equipment free of the planet. They began as tentative pokes at the outer layers of the atmosphere, but quickly burst through into outer space. Obviously, the earliest missions revealed the broadest discoveries, such as the famous Van Allen Belts: two large regions of charged particles trapped by Earth's magnetic field. These belts were detected by the first American space satellite, *Explorer 1,* launched on the last day of 1958. The belts are the only substantial fields found around any of the Terrestrial planets. *Explorer 6,* dispatched a year and a half later, returned the first television pictures of Earth.

While the manned space programs have come and gone, the *Explorers* have enjoyed the greatest longevity. These missions operated under that name until the mid-seventies, and continue on today in the spirit of many of the cooperative international ventures the U.S. has entered into with its allies. The *Explorers* probed the atmosphere and its immediate environs, tested the planet's magnetic field, and studied the effects of the Sun upon it. Just as nearly every probe ever launched has at some time turned its sensors towards the Sun, so have they looked back at Earth.

The benefits of this increased knowledge affect us in ways we may not always appreciate. With the improvements in weather forecasting alone, our greater understanding of atmospheric conditions and improved measuring devices affect us on a daily basis. More important, however, is the good this information can do for farmers, navigators, and prognosticators, among others. Perhaps the most tangible result of our recent access to space is the proliferation of communications satellites that beam the televised world into our living rooms and serve as the life blood of international business and government. (Though international spying and politically controversial projects—such as SDI—are of increasing concern.)

There is, of course, much that has been left out of this examination of Earth. Telling people about Earth is somewhat like walking into their homes and telling them about the things they have inside. Thousands of years of folklore have created a rich history of the planet we live on and our perceptions of it. It may be a case of not being able to find the forest through the trees, but seeing Earth as the planet it truly is may be impossible for all but the astronauts and cosmonauts who have had such an opportunity.

The development of life upon this planet is a story all of its own. It may be a great leap to go from the primordial soup to freeze-dried spaceship fare, but the terrain between is better covered elsewhere. The existence of human beings on Earth may well separate it from all the other planets of our solar system, but that distinction would hardly be noticeable to distant viewers. Approaching our Sun, they would first see great Jupiter in orbit. Soon thereafter Saturn would come into view, followed by the other Gas Giants. Eventually the Terrestrial planets would become noticeable, small objects orbiting within the Sun's own ring, the Asteroid Belt. Perhaps such visitors would bother to visit the noisy blue world close to the average star. They would find a truly unique planet, and perhaps they'd even find us.

A bird's-eye view of yet another extra-terrestrial mission (above) has been a frequently repeated scene. Once scientists were capable of carrying such enormous payloads safely into space, manned missions soon followed. Astronaut Ed White (opposite page) is seen during the first American space-walk. While mission commander James McDivitt remained in the craft, White's walk helped mark a new era in manned space exploration.

Neil Armstrong's "one small step for man" is forever preserved in the photo above. The footprint itself may have been blasted clean by the lunar module's return to lunar orbit, but for those who witnessed it, it left a lasting impression. The proximity of Earth and its satellite (opposite page) has created a relationship between the two that makes it impossible to consider one without the other.

The Moon

Earthlings know more about their Moon than any other astronomical body. We have poked and probed it for more than two decades, during which time we've sent crafts crashing into it, watched men step upon it, and operated cameras and buggies on its surface. And yet its history has been, and probably will be for a long time, one of myth and mystery.

While the Sun shone consistently on Earth, serving as an essential, vital force, the Moon was constantly changing its appearance. The earliest sentient creatures quickly became attuned to the cyclical nature of the Moon and relied on it for reasons both instinctual and learned. Life on Earth is inextricably involved in the planet's interaction with its Moon, yet the satellite itself is a dead world. Despite an occasional moonquake, the Moon has remained essentially quiet. Its surface consists of the scattered remnants of meteoric activity and molten flooding that occurred during its first billion or so years.

Until the telescopic era, the Moon was assumed to be a smooth, perfect ball. This fit nicely with religious doctrine and made sense to enough learned men to be deemed plausible. Englishman Thomas Harriot, not Galileo, first saw the Moon's surface in detail, a few months before the Italian did, in 1609. Galileo, however, was first to understand that a cratered lunar surface contradicted a number of widely held religious beliefs, and he managed to catch a good deal of flak in the process. The remainder of the century was spent observing and mapping this richly cratered world. While general planetary theory expanded our understanding of the Moon, it was not until the twentieth century that our lunar knowledge was greatly increased.

The Moon has always been a prime target in the minds of explorers. Jules Verne, in *A Journey to the Moon,* tried to take us there long before we were capable, but the "Space Race" (perhaps the most productive "research war" in history) quickly brought our satellite within reach. A short hop of 384 thousand kilometers away, the Moon provided an opportunity to test our hardware before venturing out into interplanetary space. After a few tentative missions were sent into Earth orbit, the Soviet space program began a series of *Luna* missions aimed at the Moon. The first, launched on the second day of 1959, missed completely but became the first satellite to leave Earth's orbit and eventually circle the Sun. The second *Luna* mission scored a bullseye, hitting the Moon nine months later. *Luna 3* returned the very first pictures from the far side.

The Americans tried to keep up with their competitors, but had a rather inauspicious beginning with the *Ranger* probes. The first one aimed at the Moon missed the distance by ten percent, and the second crashed into the Moon's far side, its systems disabled. Another miss and subsequent malfunction led mission scientists to redesign the probes. A series of kamikaze photographic missions provided thousands of new views of the lunar surface before eventually crashing into it.

Employing a landing technique that had failed for the *Ranger* probes, the Russians accomplished a soft-landing on the Moon in 1966 with *Luna 6,* after five unsuccessful attempts.

The craft returned photos from the lunar surface for three days before it failed, and its successor was the first craft to orbit the Moon. What began as a race, however, became a walkover when the U.S. showed its imminent ability to place a man on the Moon. After two years of unmanned testing, the second manned *Apollo* mission (the first to use the enormous *Saturn 5* rocket) sent three astronauts to the Moon for ten orbits during Christmas of 1968. Seven months later, on July 20th, 1969, Neil Armstrong and ''Buzz'' Aldrin walked out onto the lunar surface and ushered in a new era of scientific exploration. By the end of 1972, five more Apollo missions would study the Moon's surface. Since that time only a handful of Soviet probes, including one with a surface rover, have revisited the Moon. The *Luna* program managed to return soil samples to Earth in 1970, but despite being more relevant for future missions to nearby planets, the accomplishment was lost in the glare of Apollo's brilliant success.

While these lunar programs taught us most of what we now know about conditions on the Moon's surface, they failed to resolve the debate concerning the satellite's creation. Whether the young Moon was captured into orbit by Earth, or was at one time part of the same swirling cloud from which Earth eventually emerged, remains unresolved. If both the Moon and Earth formed from the same cloud, was it a matter of simultaneous development or the breaking away of excess matter? The fact that the Moon is slowly moving away from Earth lends credence to the idea that it originally spun off the proto-Earth. And the odds of capture make such an occurrence seem highly improbable. We should remember, however, that the solar system incorporates a great number of improbabilities.

Whatever its origin, the Moon is a dead world similar to Mercury and a number of the outer satellites. It's the fifth largest planetary moon, closest in size to the Jovian moons, Io and Europa. (All three, it happens, are the densest satellites.) It is locked into an orbit in which it rotates on its axis at the very same rate it revolves about Earth. The result of this orbit is a bulge in the shape of the Moon that perpetuates a gravitational interlock similar to that which spins Mercury about the Sun (see page 33). The relationship, however, is not totally one-sided. Over the past billion years the effect of the Moon's gravitational pull on Earth's oceans has slowed our days. Only three hundred fifty million years ago, an Earth day took twenty-two hours. In another few billion years, until the Moon eventually breaks free of Earth's gravitational control, the two will lock into a geocentric orbit. The Moon will develop an Earth day equal to fifty-five current Earth days—one that would be equal to the lunar month, with the satellite hanging permanently over one specific spot on Earth.

Our familiarity with the lunar surface has introduced us to a number of interesting geological features. Some impact craters on the small body are so wide that an astronaut standing at their center could not see the crater's walls over the horizon. The disproportionately large size of lunar features (compared to their terrestrial counterparts) is primarily due to the Moon's low gravity. Early surface anomalies were freer from the constraints of gravity, and therefore able to

Edwin "Buz" Aldrin, the second man to walk on the Moon, stands near a leg of the Apollo 11 *Lunar Module. The mission marked the culmination of a decade-long effort by the American space program to put a man on another astronomical body. The mission's success was greater than anyone could have foreseen.*

Homeward bound. As Apollo 11 headed back towards Earth it took this stunning picture of a full moon. The satellite's maria *(dark spots) and bright highlands are visible, while craters are most discernable near the edges.*

Before leaving the surface, Astronaut Aldrin (opposite page) posed for this portrait with the American flag. The site was located inside one of the dark mare *named the Sea of Tranquillity.*

move about and rise up. Meteor impacts could push the lunar surface up farther than gravity could pull it back. Cracks in the cooling surface also created large rilles (channellike features) and mountains nearly equal in size to Earth's largest ranges.

Conditions on the uneven lunar surface are particularly harsh. The Moon is a dead, airless world subject to extraordinary extremes of heat and cold. With an atmosphere a million times less than that of Earth's at sea level, the Moon is incapable of retaining the heat that scorches it during direct exposure to the Sun. Lunar high noon means temperatures above one hundred degrees Celsius, while nighttime readings are two hundred and fifty degrees lower.

And yet this drab, barren world remains a muse to a great number of earthlings. Sometimes an ephemeral sliver at dusk, other times a bold beacon shining in full splendor, the moon is idyll to romantics, guiding light for nocturnal activity, and seducer of lunatics (hence the name), as well as other things both factual and fictive. The featured performer in our night sky is the Moon, just an average planetary satellite.

In the future, earthlings may well establish permanent bases on the Moon. The turn of the next century could see research and industry prepared to embark on a new lunar era. As with the earliest unmanned probes, such missions would also serve as the perfect testing conditions for similar projects on an interplanetary scale. Once life on the Moon is shown to be feasible, Mars seems just around the corner.

MARS

DESPITE ITS RELATIVELY SMALL SIZE, MARS POSSESSES SOME OF THE MOST REMARKABLE FEATURES OF all the Terrestrial Planets. Massive volcanoes, enormous canyons, and catastrophic flood plains are scattered across a planet half the diameter of Earth, more comparable in size to Mercury and the Moon. As probes familiarized us with these Martian wonders during the 1960s and 1970s, scientists and the public discovered a fascinating planet, devoid of the life we had hoped to find but rich in surface features beyond our imagination.

Among Mars' most prominent features, the Olympus Mons is the largest volcanic mountain in the known solar system. Dwarfing any found on Earth or Venus, Olympus is a shield volcano, rising twenty kilometers above the surface and radiating out to encompass an area the size of Arizona. A series of companion volcanoes found on a plain called the Tharsis Bulge is also greater than any such assemblage on Earth. They sit on Mars' unshifting surface above a region of great internal activity. (On Earth, shifting tectonic plates prevent any one area from receiving the complete force of the localized internal activity, while a single-plate surface, such as Mars', is incapable of such movement.)

Mars' enormous volcanic regions, such as the Tharsis Bulge seen here from the first Viking orbiter in 1980, feature extinct volcanoes standing 17 kilometers above a prominent plateau.

Farther away from the planet (opposite page), the Viking spacecraft assembled this image of the Red Planet. The starry background is an artist's enhancement, but the pocked and wrinkled surface is truly Mars' own.

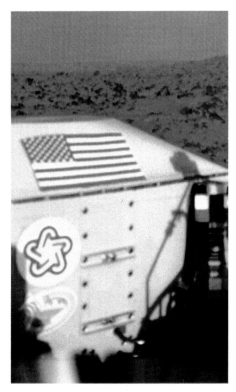

Early morning, July 26th, Martian Standard Time. The U.S. flag provides identifiable colors against which the Martian surface can be compared. Two weeks after America's Bicentennial (celebrated by the logo seen beneath the flag), Viking became the first man-made craft to touch down on Mars.

Equally gargantuan is a canyon of chaotic terrain and long-dry water beds, the Valleris Marineris. An enormous gash running parallel to Mars' equator, the Valleris defies any Earthly comparisons; our own Grand Canyon is equivalent to only one of its unnamed tributaries. The Martian canyon cuts across four thousand kilometers of the surface—about the distance from New York to San Diego—which is the entire length of the diminutive planet's radius.

The Valleris was named in honor of the *Mariner 9* craft that discovered it in 1971. The probe was the first to orbit another planet, a far cry from the fleeting glimpses of earlier flybys such as *Mariner 4*. In 1964, that early mission passed within ten thousand kilometers of Mars before hurtling off into uncharted space. Limited in the amount of the Martian terrain it could photograph, what the *Mariner 4* was able to transmit back happened to be particularly heavily cratered. This originally led scientists to believe Mars had much in common with Mercury and the Moon. Two subsequent *Mariner* flybys passed along similar findings, fostering a misleading image of Martian topography that remained until the extensive mapping and photographing conducted by *Mariner 9*.

However misleading the early *Mariner* results may have been, they were certainly much closer to the truth than the wishful thinking and ridiculous proposals of the earliest astronomers. By now we are all familiar with the "canals" thought to criss-cross Mars—"obvious" signs of a burgeoning civilization, inherently aggressive like the god of war for whom the planet was named. In 1877, Italian astronomer Giovanni Schiaparelli completed his studies of a Martian surface covered with *canali*. Though the Italian word is actually the equivalent of the English word channels, it was corrupted into canals, implying artificial objects dug by (who else?) Martians.

The championing of intelligent life on Mars was taken up in the United States by a wealthy Bostonian, Percival Lowell. He established a state-of-the-art observatory in Flagstaff, Arizona with the specific intention of confirming Schiaparelli's findings. While the Lowell Observatory did lead serious astronomers to a great many discoveries, the zealotry of its builder helped cloud the public's perception of Mars for a long, long time. Throughout the twentieth century Mars has figured prominently in tales of interplanetary hostility and extra-terrestrial attacks. Accorded the attributes of mythological Mars, the blood red planet inspired H.G. Wells' *War of the Worlds* and scores of other imaginative invasions. An impressive assortment, in fact, for a lifeless world of dust storms and permafrost.

It wasn't until the first probes passed Mars, however, that scientists could offer strong alternatives to the fictional scenarios popularized elsewhere. In the early 1960s both the Soviets and Americans aimed their rockets towards the red planet, only to meet with varying levels of failure. The first Mars-bound *Mariner* mission launched by the U.S. was a failure, as was Russia's *Mars 1*. The U.S. eventually found success with the previously mentioned *Mariner* follow-ups, while the U.S.S.R. met with an embarrassing series of failures throughout the early 1970s. Capsules failed to enter Mars' orbit, crashed into its surface, or missed the planet completely.

While America's *Viking* missions have gathered their deserved acclaim as the first objects to return useful data from the planet's surface, Russia's *Mars 3* had landed on the planet five years earlier. Unfortunately, that lander transmitted data for only twenty seconds before malfunctioning, its photographic capabilities never realized.

In the summer of 1976, Martian studies reached a peak with the arrival of *Viking 1* and *Viking 2*. Each mission included an orbiter and a lander, the latter to take photographs and analyze samples of the planet's surface. *Viking 1* touched down on Mars on July 20, 1976, the seventh anniversary of *Apollo 11*'s landing on the Moon. It returned photos of a rubble-strewn, salmon pink surface against a light pink sky, thus giving Mars the name red planet. (Mars' atmosphere is too thin to account for any substantial refraction of sunlight, leading scientists to conclude that the sky's pink tint is caused by the oxidized Martian dust kicked up above the planet's surface by atmospheric currents.)

An expensive stereopticon: This overlapping image was made by two cameras on the Viking *lander, which allows scientists to create three-dimensional images of the Martian surface. The view features the horizon from the landing site on the Chryse Planitia.*

The many faces of Mars: Using a variety of lenses, enhancements, and exposures, spacecrafts have provided us with colorful views of our neighbor.

The top photo on this page uses computer-generated, false-color enhancement of the Martian surface. Color variations are exaggerated to provide scientists with a better understanding of subtle differences between types of clouds or rock materials.

Another computer enhanced photograph (below), depicts a time-lapse Martian sunset as the planet falls into darkness. Microscopic atmospheric dust is responsible for the blue cast seen beneath the Sun; these particles are similar to those that make Earth's sky so blue.

The second Viking orbiter captured this image of dawn on Mars during its approach to the planet. The great Valles Marineris can be seen running horizontally across the lower portion of the visible surface. To its left is Ascreaus Mons, one of Mars' enormous volcanoes.

Olympus Mons, the largest known volcano in the solar system, is seen here in an artist's rendering, based on photographs returned from Mariner 9. The base of this enormous structure is 600 kilometers across, and its peak rises 25 kilometers above the planet's surface.

Viking 2 landed two months later, at a sight farther north. Scientists had chosen its destination based on aerial data that suggested greater moisture in the area. Despite the technological advancements necessary for such a mission, the landing sight was chosen in search of the one thing man had hoped to discover for centuries: life on Mars. No longer expecting malicious monsters or evil empires, scientists were still clinging to the notion that life of some basic kind might exist there. A series of complex experiments were developed to determine whether small microorganisms might occur in the damp layer of soil at the planet's surface. Initial tests were sufficiently inconclusive to give some hope, but a final search for traces of life-related organic compounds seemed negative enough to override any of the earlier results.

While the landers studied the surface, one of the *Viking* orbiters was able to focus its attention elsewhere. The first continued to relay data received from the two landers, while the other was reprogrammed to study the planet's polar caps. Even the earliest Earth-based studies had confirmed the presence of such frozen regions, and more powerful telescopes indicated a cycle of seasonal changes.

The *Viking* missions uncovered the mystery of Mars' fluctuating polar caps, which did, in fact, consist of large amounts of frozen water. Their growth during the winter seasons, however, was determined to be the condensation of carbon dioxide into dry ice. These discoveries were tied into a complex system of atmospheric patterns not all that dissimilar to those on Earth. *Viking*'s tracking of trans-global windstorms also led scientists such as Carl Sagan to consider the possibility of a "nuclear winter" on Earth based on some of the properties discovered during Martian dust storms. (One storm raged with such intensity that early photographs transmitted from *Mariner 9* were unable to penetrate the dust clouds to register any surface features. Scientists feared the entire mission might be obscured, but the storm lifted in time for the probe's historic discoveries.)

In addition to their atmospheric studies, the *Viking* orbiters transmitted thousands of high-resolution photographs of the planet's surface. Those photos suggested that the presence of

Considered by many to be evidence of running water at some point in the Martian past, lengthy channels, hundreds of kilometers long, can be found across the planet's surface. This artist's rendering depicts a channel about five kilometers across, winding its way north of the planet's equator.

Viewed from above, the Martian channels crisscross the surface in testament to a wetter past. Today, Mars is drier than the Sahara Desert, its only available water found in the ground ice. This image, obtained from the Viking *1 orbiter in 1980, focuses on the planet's Mangala Vallis region.*

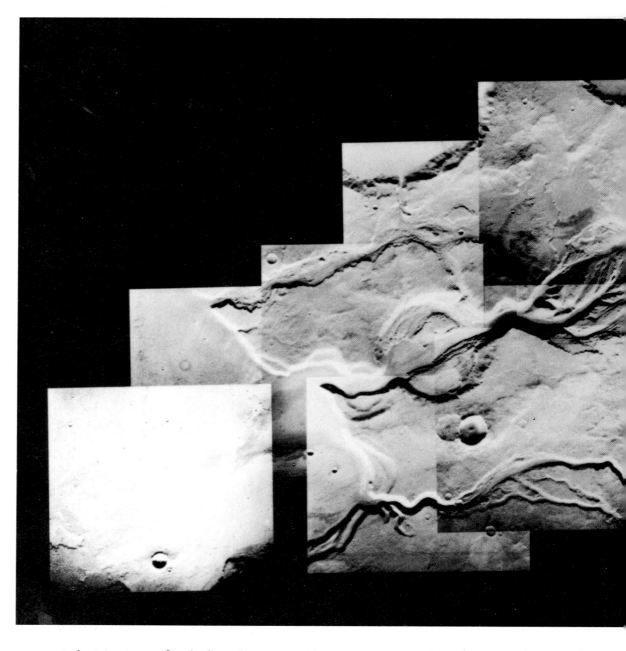

water on the Martian surface had not been a singular occurrence. Geologic features indicative of flowing water were long thought to have formed during one specific period in Mars' past, before most of the liquid was locked into the permafrost that pervades the planet's surface. (Calculations indicate that were it to melt, there is enough frozen water on the planet to cover its surface with an ocean kilometers deep.) Images from *Viking,* however, showed levels of water erosion in a variety of relationships, with periods of cratering and volcanic activity. The current belief is that a few hundred million years ago Mars may have been warm enough—probably from heat generated within—to straddle the melting point. Seasonal, orbital, and internal changes

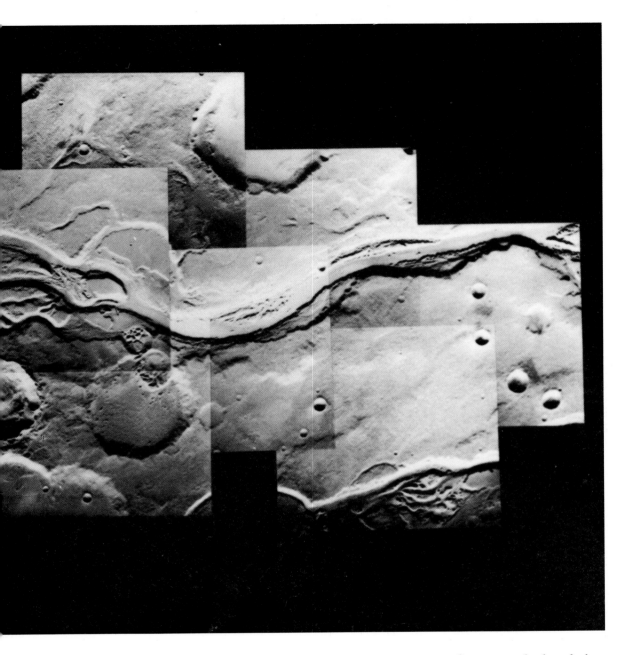

could have combined to create conditions in which vast amounts of water melted and then refroze, unleashing a series of catastrophic floods.

While the presence of flowing water in the Martian past goes a long way toward explaining a number of the planet's surface features, it also serves to reawaken the oldest of all debates about the planet. Creating a scenario of catastrophic floods and running rivers, scientists began to consider the possibility that such conditions could have supported life at an earlier time. Unable to prove its present existence, theorists have turned to the past in their dwindling hope that life, in some form or another, might once have existed on the planet.

The Moons of Mars

In 1610 the German astronomer and theorist, Johannes Kepler, predicted the existence of a pair of moons circling Mars. He couldn't find them, but felt certain that they were there. A century later, novelist Jonathan Swift presumed their existence in *Gulliver's Travels,* although actual confirmation would not arrive until 1877. It was then, during a period of particularly close proximity to Mars, that an American, Asaph Hall, discovered a pair of rocky objects spinning quickly about Mars.

Hall, using the U.S. Naval Observatory in Washington, might have preferred naming at least one of the newly discovered moons after his wife, whom he credited with convincing him to persevere in his search. But following the established tradition, he named them after mythological characters, selecting Phobos—god of fear and alarm—and Deimos—god of terror—both sons of Ares, Mars' Greek equivalent. Phobos, the larger of the two, is a mere twenty-seven kilometers across, comparable in length to Manhattan Island. Deimos measures a mere fifteen

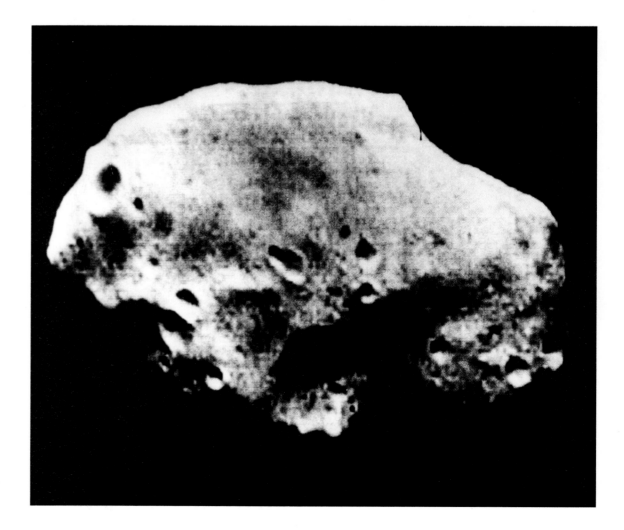

Phobos, the larger of the Martian moons, was photographed by Mariner 9 from 5,500 kilometers away as it orbited the planet. Numerous craters are visible, indicating that the moon is probably quite old and strong enough to have weathered a great beating. Many scientists believe the two Martian moons are the sole survivors of a larger group.

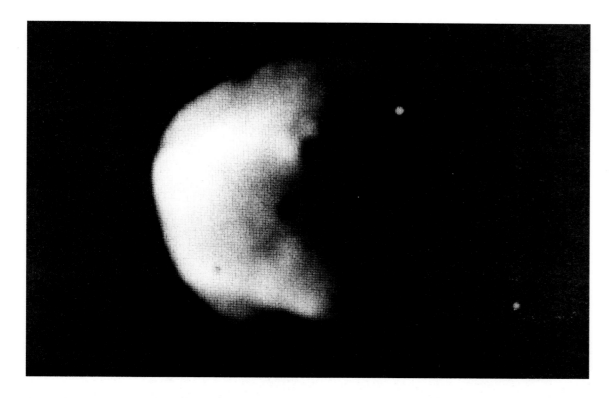

Deimos, considerably smaller than its partner, was little more than a blur in these photographs sent from Mariner 9 in 1971. A future Soviet mission hopes to undertake the closest examination of both Martian moons to date.

kilometers across. (Moons of similar size around the outer Gas Giants have often found themselves consigned to simple numerical assignations or generalized groupings; thousands of asteroids this size remain uncharted and unnamed. Perhaps only their early discovery and proximity to Earth prompted discoverers to name the two moons so quickly.)

While our own Earth/Moon partnership is actually closer to a double-planet system, Mars' moons are similar to many of those circling the outer planets. Their orbits are short, their gravities are nearly nonexistent, and their masses are a tiny fraction of their host's. Both Phobos and Deimos are cratered, fragmented chunks of rock, with properties that suggest greater similarity to asteroids than any planetoid structures.

Any guess as to the origin and make-up of the Martian satellites is now superfluous, because of the impending arrival of the Soviet probes scheduled to rendezvous with them shortly. Hovering within fifty kilometers of Phobos' surface, the first probe will direct a laser blast at it, analyzing the resulting debris before attempting a tricky landing on the small moon itself. If that mission proves successful, a second probe will attempt a similar survey of Deimos.

The information from this and future missions could answer many questions about the Martian moons, particularly concerning their origin. While some scientists believe them to have been captured asteroids, others claim the two to be the sole remaining members of a once crowded ring, since scattered from Mars' domain. A successful Soviet mission will redefine our conceptions of Phobos and Deimos, two intriguing little bodies passing quickly across the Martian sky.

Manned or unmanned, any attempt to return samples of the Martian soil to Earth would probably follow the steps depicted in this drawing. Though the actual capsules may not exactly resemble those shown here, their departure and return to an orbiting craft will be quite similar.

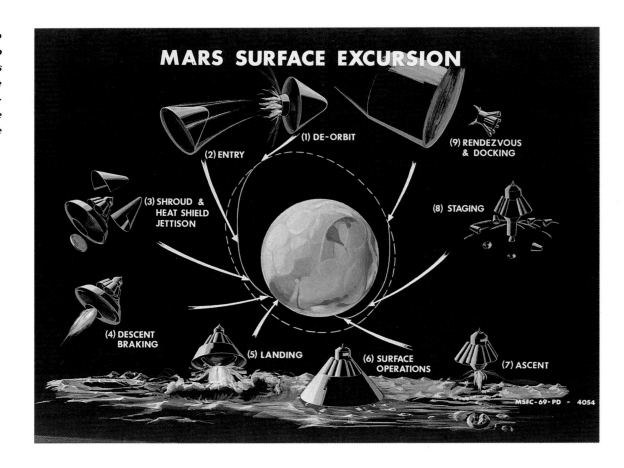

These days, any discussion of future manned explorations points to Mars. Its proximity to Earth and comparatively hospitable environment have made it a prime focus in the long-term planning of Soviet, American, and European space programs. The Soviet mission to the Martian moons will also gather data on the planet for future missions. Soon thereafter, in 1992 or '94, the Soviets hope to land a craft on the surface of Mars to conduct further experiments on the planet's soil. The United States space program had hoped to launch a Mars Observer to return data on geologic and climactic conditions in 1990, but has since postponed the mission until 1992 at the earliest.

Most ambitious of all is a Soviet project planned for 1996 or 1998. It hopes to deposit a lander on the Martian surface that will ferry soil samples to an orbiting device for their transportation to Earth and first-hand examination. At this time it offers the greatest opportunity for direct study of the Martian surface in this century. (The biennial nature of these projected missions is due to the fact that Mars takes two years to orbit the Sun, bringing it closest to Earth that often as well. The planets close to within 52 million kilometers of each other at these times, recurring in cycles of fifteen and seventeen years. The next such favorable opposition, in the year 2003, may prove a bit early for a manned mission, but suggests a period of time when doing so would be made easier.)

Into the next century, Mars certainly appears the odds-on favorite for manned travel to another planet. Long the hope of idealists and science fiction writers, the concept of a manned base on Mars sounds increasingly feasible. The nature of such a lengthy and complex mission, however, has presented a number of challenges to the nations of the world. The return of cosmonaut Yuri Romanenko in December of 1987, after eleven months in Earth orbit, made it obvious that prolonged visits to outer space are still considerably detrimental to human health.

Until now, collaboration among the leaders in space exploration has been minimal at best. Yet the more we come to understand the complex logistics of a manned mission to Mars, the more essential it seems. As long as nations feel a need to be secretive about their space technology—usually due to militaristic concerns—it is unlikely that we will see much camaraderie among them. The race to Mars could well parallel the earliest, coldest stages of the ''Space Race.'' The potential exists for the aggressive spirit of the deadly god of war to appear if space travel is pursued separately and competitively. Instead, the exploration of Mars could usher in a new generation of men and women coming together as representatives of a united planet.

A return of samples from the Martian surface will mark still another era in the exploration of space. Perhaps then the question of life on Mars could finally be put to rest, allowing scientists to get on with further studies of the planet's soil.

MSFC-69-PD - 4053

The initial search that uncovered the existence of the asteroid belt was a primitive affair, employing equipment such as that used in the Old Observing Room at the Greenwich Observatory (right).

Today, technology has made it possible to take a closer look at the asteroids themselves. This artist's rendering (opposite page) envisions a shuttle-launched craft entering into the belt to actually retrieve an asteriod for closer examination.

THE ASTEROID BELT

DURING THE EARLIEST STAGES OF TELESCOPIC ASTRONOMY, A NUMBER OF "COMPREHENSIVE" LAWS were created in an attempt to establish some kind of uniformity in the solar system. In 1772, the Titius-Bode law tried to assign numerical values to the known planets in relation to their distance from the Sun. The law made great sense to many, but it had the disadvantage of being unable to account for the lack of a planet between Mars and Jupiter. As a result, some scientists remained skeptical; the discovery of Uranus swayed many. Its distance from the Sun was remarkably close to where the Titius-Bode law would have predicted, lending the theory greater credence.

Towards the end of the eighteenth century, a "Celestial Police" was established by a group of astronomers to search for the missing world out past Mars. They were, however, beaten to the discovery by an Italian astronomer, Giuseppe Piazzi, who spoted Ceres on the first day of 1801. It came to be considered a minor planet, and the answer to the Celestial Police's search. Thus, the Titius-Bode law became an established part of the astronomical canon, although it didn't account for the other minor planets that began to pop up soon thereafter. Over the next few years, Pallas, Juno, and Vesta followed the discovery of Ceres—all four of them tiny, sub-planetary objects which are now known as asteroids.

The word asteroid was coined by Uranus-discoverer, Sir William Herschel, and refers to a star-like object. At the time of their discovery even the strongest telescopes of the day were unable to discern any shape to the asteroids, leaving them points of light like the stars (whereas planets offer a discernable disk through telescopes). The largest asteroid, Ceres, measures a mere thousand kilometers across, while the thousands of asteroids discovered since have included some as small as one kilometer in size. Some asteroids are minor planets, similar in mass to the smaller moons, while others have collided amongst themselves so often that they are reduced to their

North Wind Picture Archives

metallic cores. Combined, all the asteroids together still account for less than a tenth of the Moon's mass.

Originally, theorists believed that a legitimate planet had once existed in the asteroid belt. Our current understanding, however, indicates that the effect of Jupiter's enormous mass on the planetesimals prevented them from ever coalescing in the first place. The giant planet stole much of the loose matter that would have been needed for the creation of a separate planet and stirred up the orbits of the remaining asteroids to prevent them from ever coming together.

The result is a collection of small rocky particles in random orbit around the Sun. While the majority maintain orbits within those of Mars and Jupiter, smaller groups are known to have more eccentric paths. Some asteroids have been tracked farther out in the solar system, such as Chiron, discovered in 1977. Traveling out beyond Saturn, it will probably be flung from the solar system a few million years from now when its eccentric orbit carries it beyond the Sun's domain. Closer in, asteroids have been known to travel within the orbits of Venus, Mercury, and Earth.

When these small groups of asteroids approach Earth's orbit, we often witness spectacular meteor showers. Occasionally, however, asteroids large enough to survive the plunge through our atmosphere become meteorites. At their largest, they can be quite destructive. Some scientists believe that one period of particular intensity may have been responsible for the extinction of dinosaurs and that another, expected to pass in about fifteen-and-a-half million years, could well jeopardize our own existence. (Proponents of "Nemesis," the Sun's suggested binary companion, see that object as responsible for the orbit of this deadly band of asteroids.) While it may be a bit early for panic, a greater understanding of these stray asteroid groups and their erratic orbits could prove quite helpful to future generations.

PART III

The
GAS GIANTS...
AND PLUTO

With the Gas Giants it is necessary to imagine these planets on a much greater scale than their Terrestrial counterparts. All four of the actual Giants are shown to be considerably larger in the top diagram (opposite page, top), while below it shows the path of Voyager 2. Through it and its predecessor, our understanding of the outer members of our solar system has grown exponentially.

Out past the asteroid belt, the planets of the solar system take on a whole new set of dimensions. The scale with which we examined the Terrestrial Planets must be discarded for one that can be used to understand the Gas Giants: enormous bodies that dwarf Earth and its neighbors. Far from the Sun, these planets were able to exert greater control over nearby matter than the Sun during the formative stages of the solar system. Their size is limited solely by the amount of gas available, and they are less susceptible to the Sun's gravitational force and its T Tauri housecleaning.

While the Terrestrial Planets were formed by heated rocks, attracting more of the same, the Gas Giants are believed to have begun as frozen snowballs of gaseous matter. Lighter matter—such as ammonia and water vapor—was blown from the inner planets, while those distant enough from the proto-Sun were able to keep hold of it. They quickly grew more gravitationally attractive to the surrounding region of the pre-solar nebula, drawing in more of the matter we find in their present compositions.

The closest of the Gas Giants, Jupiter and Saturn, were able to draw from enormous quantities of matter, while those farther out in the fledgling solar system were limited by the thinning cloud of gas. All have developed miniature ''solar systems'' of their own, surrounded by numerous satellites and rings not all that different from the asteroid belt. All the Giants are considerably bigger than any of the Terrestrials and shrouded by thick atmospheres that give way to uncertain surfaces. Only recently have we come to understand more about these distant wonders, and what we have learned has raised as many questions as answers.

And then there's Pluto, misfit of the solar system. Closer in size to the Terrestrials and some of the Giants' moons, it sticks out as the sole exception to any discussion of the Gas Giants. Perhaps it's an escaped moon from one of its neighbors or the runt of the litter—a barren core of a planet left underfed at the fringe of the proto-solar system. We know less about this cold, distant planet than any other member of the Sun's family, and have little prospect of learning much more in the near future. Whether it's the final outpost of the Sun's domain, or one of several dead worlds scattered across the edges of the solar system, remains to be seen. In the meantime, we watch the distant planet in hopes of unraveling the riddles of its past and present.

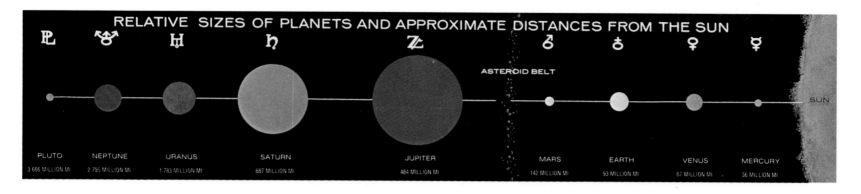

RELATIVE SIZES OF PLANETS AND APPROXIMATE DISTANCES FROM THE SUN

ASTEROID BELT

SUN

PLUTO	NEPTUNE	URANUS	SATURN	JUPITER	MARS	EARTH	VENUS	MERCURY
3,666 MILLION MI	2,795 MILLION MI	1,783 MILLION MI	887 MILLION MI	484 MILLION MI	142 MILLION MI	93 MILLION MI	67 MILLION MI	36 MILLION MI

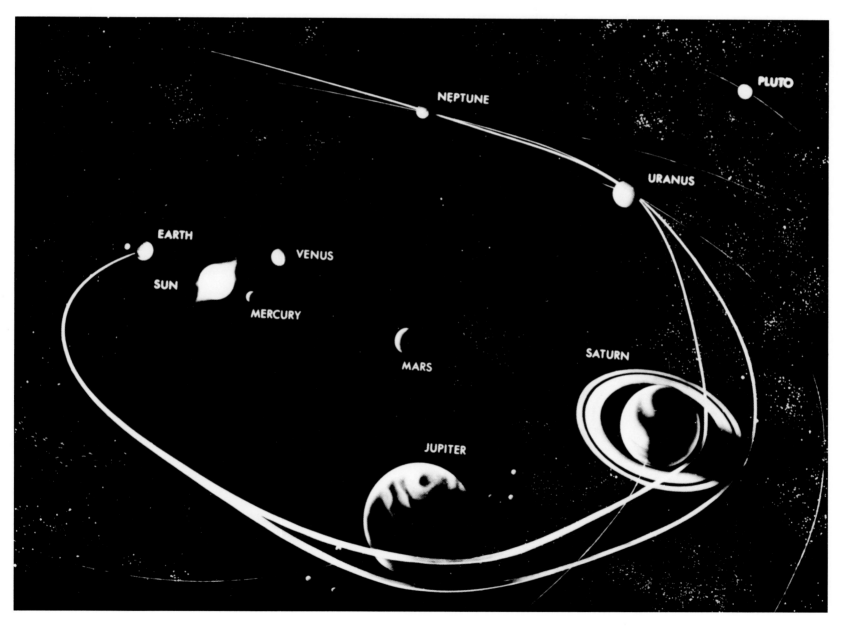

JUPITER

JUPITER IS BIG. THERE IS LITTLE IN OUR LIVES OR OUR EXPERIENCES THAT PREPARES US TO comprehend the size of such a planet. Were Jupiter any bigger it would be a star, and there are some who nearly consider it one. Whether it's a massive planet or a brown dwarf—a potential binary companion to the Sun that failed to ignite—is up for debate. Either way it's big.

Appropriately named for the king of all gods, Jupiter reigns supreme among the planets. It keeps the inner planets tightly within the ecliptic plane, and a solar system's worth of moons in an even tighter orbit around it. We know of more Jovian moons than planets, and knew of the largest of them before having discovered Uranus, Neptune, and Pluto. And in studying Jupiter's relationship with its satellites we have come to better understand the relationships between the Sun and the planets.

A Voyager-eye view of Jupiter. Both photos of Jupiter have been enhanced, but draw on images from the Voyager crafts. The composite below features the planet and its four largest moons— Io, Europa, Ganymede, and Callisto— best known as the Galilean moons.

The discovery of those moons by Galileo is oft told, as is his use of their presence to conclude the heliocentric nature of the solar system. His discovery got Galileo into trouble with the Catholic Church, but it cemented the idea into serious scientific minds. In all fairness, a German named Simon Marius had spotted the largest Jovian moons days before Galileo, and he was allowed to assign them their names. Marius, however, failed to connect the observation with its greater implications.

The logic proceeds that if Jupiter had moons revolving around it, then those objects did not rely on Earth as the center of their orbit—indicating that perhaps Earth did not occupy the center of the solar system. Galileo was lucky to have been the first to train the newly invented telescope upon so many objects in the night sky. By connecting the implications of the phases of the inner planets, the cratering of the Moon, the orbits of the Jovian moons, and other phenomena, Galileo was afforded the best clues to the heliocentricity of the solar system. Today, we have learned nearly as much about the Jovian moons as we have about Jupiter itself. Among the four Galilean moons (as they have come to be known), we find a diverse lot with very different "personalities." Were there intelligent life on the king of the planets, it wouldn't be hard to imagine a book like this one that focused on the *Jovian* System.

Since Galileo, the great planet Jupiter has often found itself taking a back seat to its own satellites. Recent missions have created as much excitement over the volcanic activity on Io and the possibility of life on Europa as they have for anything on the planet around which they revolve. So, before becoming sidetracked by the alluring system that surrounds it, let's pay Jupiter its due.

The planet is predominantly composed of hydrogen and helium, with the possible exception of a small, rocky core of iron and silicates. Despite being 1300 times larger than Earth, Jupiter only weighs 318 times as much; its total density is barely greater than water's. From our vantage, the planet begins as a layer of clouds, hundreds of kilometers thick. Ultra-light layers of trace elements such as methane and ammonia skirt across the higher altitudes, held among the clouds by the retentive force of Jupiter's mass. Further into the planet it might be possible to cross through some clouds of H_2O that would eventually give way to hydrogen compressed to the point of taking on liquid properties. This is a state known as liquid molecular hydrogen, where a descending space capsule would need to be a pretty good submarine as well. There is no clear boundary between the two, no distinct surface as on Earth. In this respect, Jupiter more closely resembles the Sun than its fellow planets.

It's as we start getting close to the center of the planet that its chemical makeup begins to change. The pressure is so great that the hydrogen takes on properties normally ascribed to metals. It's not solid, but dense enough to account for three-quarters of Jupiter's mass and responsible for the planet's enormous magnetic field. The currents generated when the liquid metallic hydrogen spins rapidly at the center of the planet act like an enormous dynamo. The result is a region similar to Earth's Van Allen Belt, only greater in diameter than the Sun itself.

Another composite of the principal members of the Jovian system includes Io in the foreground. The contrast between it, the other satellites, and Jupiter itself is just one reason the system remains the most fascinating in planetary astronomy.

More than two-and-a-half million kilometers away, the Great Red Spot still looms large on the face of Jupiter. Voyager 1 captured the storm and its turbulent surroundings during its approach to the planet, before slingshotting past for a rendezvous with Saturn.

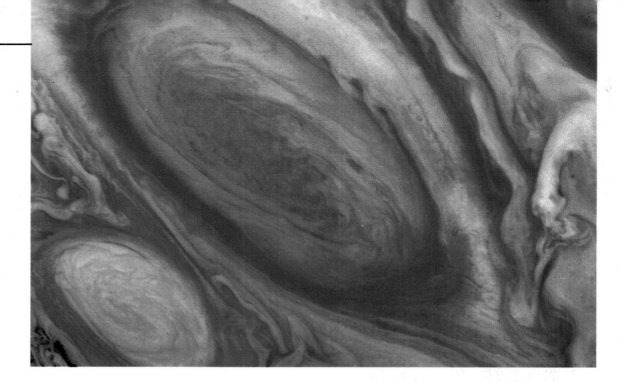

That gargantuan magnetosphere is distorted by the force of the solar wind, creating a magnetotail (a magnetic field elongated by an oncoming wind) extending to the orbit of Saturn. We have only begun to understand the total extent of its influence.

Jupiter, despite its enormous mass, turns faster than any of the other planets. It rotates in just under ten hours, though like the Sun the outer regions lag behind the inner. As a result, Jupiter is distended at the equator, its surfaceless mass swelling up at the center by drawing down from the poles. (While it may seem a matter of semantics, Jupiter's poles haven't flattened, its equator got wider.) That oblate shape is responsible for keeping Jupiter's wobble on its axis to a minimum. (A mere three degrees of tilt is maximum for Jupiter, compared to the more than twenty-three degrees of variation that account for Earth's seasons.) The distortion of the polar region also disrupts the neatly defined atmospheric zones found in the lower latitudes, by turning them into seas of swirling eddies flowing slowly behind the equatorial currents. We have learned much about the atmospheric conditions of Jupiter from the *Voyager* probes, which have taught us that Jupiter is more intricate than its banded appearance had indicated.

The best known of Jupiter's atmospheric activities is, of course, the Great Red Spot—an unimaginatively named storm of truly epic proportions that has raged for the past few centuries. In 1974, *Pioneer 10* established the fact that it was an atmospheric phenomenon, with no roots to the liquid portions of the planet below. The anticyclone (the name, in accordance with terminology used for meteorological phenomena here on Earth, means that it travels counterclockwise in the planet's southern hemisphere) sits kilometers above its neighboring clouds and leaves a wake that extends nearly halfway back around the planet. *Voyager* discovered that the outer edges of the spot rotated around a nearly stationary center in six days. The spot is so large that three Earths could fit in it.

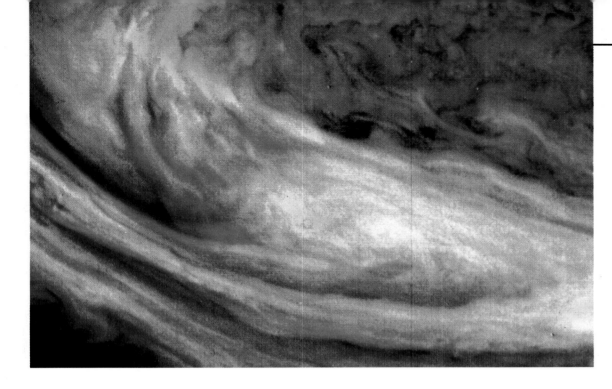

An exaggeration of color differences allows the true fury of activity within the Great Red Spot (left) to be seen more clearly.

An artificially created composite (below) shows the difference between the size of Earth and the Red Spot, itself just a small part of the enormous planet.

Many of the peculiarities in the Jovian atmosphere are due to the fact that the planet's surface receives more heat from below than from the Sun. As the enormous planet continues to contract, the pressure on the center generates a great deal of heat. Therefore, considerations of Jupiter's atmospheric patterns need to include convection currents coming from below (like the Sun) as well as the kind of atmospheric activities found on the Terrestrial Planets.

The study of Jupiter remained Earth-based for a long time. Only once NASA had established its ability to conduct successful missions to the nearby planets could a treacherous journey through the asteroid belt be attempted. If sand-sized grains of interplanetary dust occupied the space between the more easily detected asteroids, a probe would be useless at the speeds necessary for its journey. As a result, the first missions to Jupiter were more concerned with surviving than surveying. Equipped with a television camera and little else, *Pioneer 10* sped by the planet in December 1973, before darting into uncharted space. The next *Pioneer* included Saturn on its itinerary, but still pales in comparison to the laboratories packed into the *Voyager* probes.

The *Voyager* missions were the most successful unmanned probes launched to date, totally revamping our perceptions of the largest members of the solar system. In addition to being responsible for the overwhelming majority of our knowledge about Jupiter and Saturn, almost everything we know about Uranus and everything we'll soon know of Neptune will come from *Voyager 2*. Both of the missions began with Jupiter, shedding great light on the king and its subjects. While several of *Voyager*'s major discoveries were related to the planet's satellites, the probe also discovered a Jovian ring.

After having discovered a ring around Uranus rather by chance, astronomers began to wonder whether all the Gas Giants might not possess some minor ring system. They knew the rings around Jupiter wouldn't be as breathtaking as Saturn's, but the *Voyager* missions offered an opportunity to test the theory. Catching a photographic glimpse with *Voyager 1*, scientists programmed a more extensive examination into the second probe. In the process of discovering a ring of frozen particles circling Jupiter, astronomers discovered another three moons; the tally is currently seventeen. Two of the moons shepherd the outer edge of the ring, creating a hard edge. The ring diminishes as it closes in on Jupiter itself, though it's possible there is no specific inner boundary, but a gradation from the ring to the upper levels of the planet's atmosphere.

In the same way that the cratered surfaces of Mercury and the Moon shed light on the early periods of the solar system's history, the composition of Jupiter offered scientists an opportunity to indirectly study the primordial cloud that created the Sun and planets. The tremendous mass of Jupiter manages to serve as a time capsule for the proto-solar nebula. The abundance of hydrogen and its proportionality to helium are considered to reflect that of our solar system's formative matter. Soon a probe will enter Jupiter's atmosphere and transmit to an orbiter as it descends through unexplored territory. NASA's oft-delayed *Galileo* mission is scheduled for departure in the near future. When it finally reaches the Jovian system in the middle of the next decade, it will open the next chapter in planetary exploration.

Another computer-enhanced photograph (opposite page) manages to capture the great activity taking place throughout the Jovian atmosphere. This photograph, taken by Voyager 2 *in 1979, is as aesthetically pleasing as it is scientifically informative.*

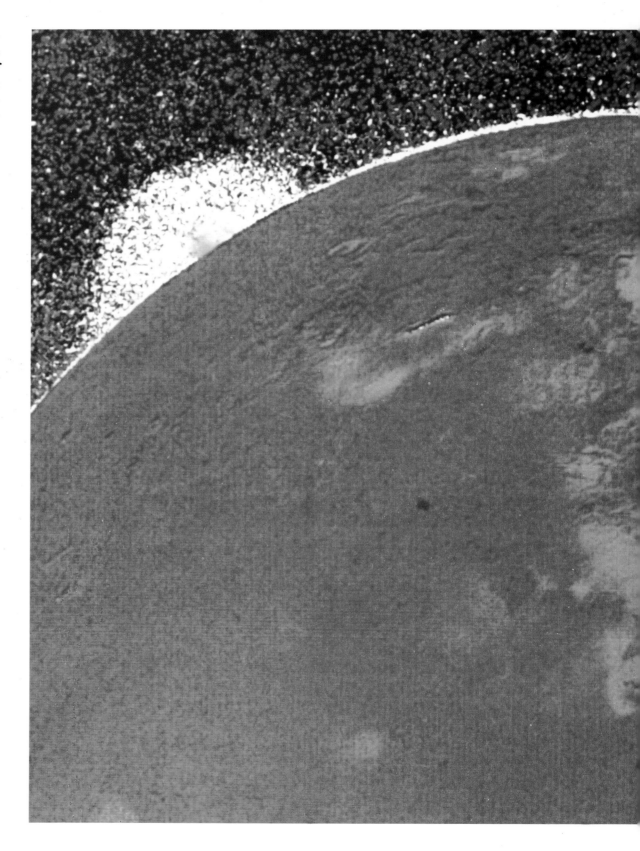

Exposures using ultraviolet and visible light were combined by Voyager 1 to provide this startling photograph of Io's volcanic activity. It was the first time scientists had the opportunity to directly view such phenomena on another astronomic body.

When the *Galileo* craft finally reaches its destination, a great deal of attention will be paid to Jupiter's many moons. As mentioned, they have become the subjects of intense scrutiny. The largest and most interesting moons are the Galileans. Io, Europa, Ganymede, and Callisto rival the Terrestrials in diversity and activity. Their orbits are all within a radius of two million kilometers, traveling in the same direction as Jupiter's rotation.

Ganymede is the largest of the moons, recently confirmed to be even bigger than Saturn's moon, Titan. Ganymede is bigger than both Mercury and Pluto, but it is lighter, since it's made of mostly water-ice. Well worn from the earliest days of bombardment, the moon gives indications of fault systems unlike any but those found on Earth and of possible tectonic activity earlier in its history. "If they were sitting around the Sun," said one *Galileo* scientist, "we'd be flying missions directly to Ganymede or Io."

Io became the early highlight of the *Voyager 1* mission when it noticed volcanic activity on Io's surface. This was the first time probes had ever witnessed such an event actually occurring. (Earlier crafts had registered indications of such activities, but had never directly recorded one.) The satellite is subject to a tug of war in its orbit around Jupiter, its surface pulled and twisted by conflicting attractions to Europa and Ganymede. This helps heat the moon's interior and crack its surface to allow geysers of sulfuric fire.

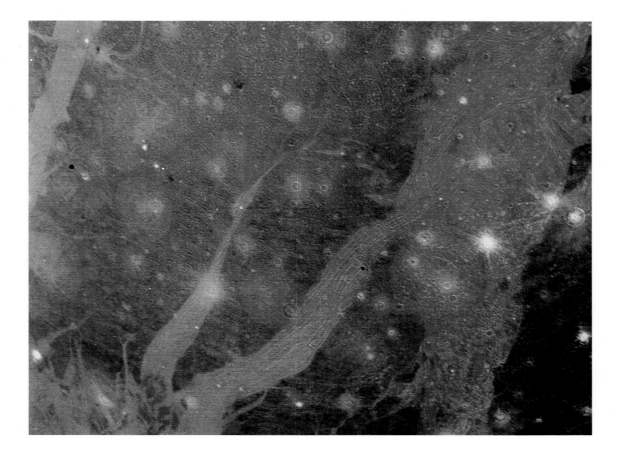

Battered Ganymede shows evidence of continued assault. The bright "halos" that can be seen scattered across the moon's surface represent recent impacts. The more linear bright sections are believed to be a result of surface movement caused by the interaction of gravitational forces between itself, Jupiter, and the other moons.

Mosaics taken four months apart (the first by Voyager 1, the second by Voyager 2) illustrate the constant change taking place on Io's surface. Volcanic activity keeps Io's surface in turmoil, constantly reestablishing it as the youngest in the solar system.

Io's surface is considered the youngest in the galaxy, the subject of extensive recent volcanism. Its constant spewing helps maintain an atmosphere that introduces the majority of new material into the Jovian system and also makes Io a recent photographic favorite in planetary astronomy. In addition to its fascinating surface, Io has a peculiar relationship with Jupiter itself; the small satellite is on the receiving end of a magnetic flow between the two. Caught in a still uncertain quirk of Jupiter's magnetic field, the moon operates as some collection point of the energy emanating from the planet.

In stark contrast to Io, Callisto, the second largest of the moons, is considered to possess the oldest surface in the solar system. Dormant since birth, Callisto remained frozen from an early age. The earliest periods of meteoric bombardment were preserved by a layer of dirty ice that later melted to cushion the force of subsequent impacts. One specific impact, however, is

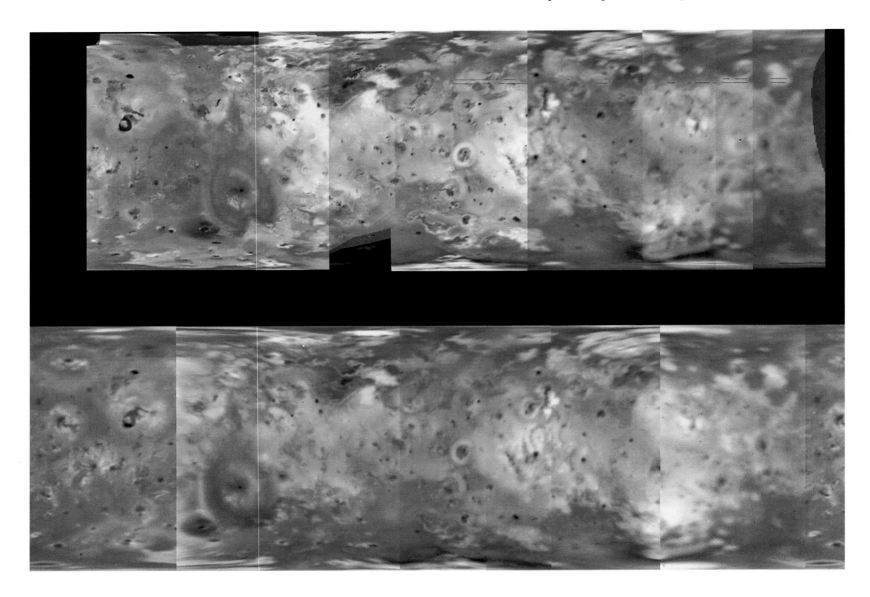

reminiscent of Mercury's Caloris Basin and worth noting. An enormous bull's-eye series of ripples radiate from a crater christened Valhalla. Ten concentric rings extend from the center, frozen for ages as the heat of the shockwaves diminished, and the ice refroze in mid-ripple.

Which leaves Europa, the fourth of the Galilean moons. Another frozen world—photographs of this satellite had always indicated extensive cracks along its surface—indicative of the kind of frozen wastelands found on Callisto, Ganymede, or in Saturn's system. But the intriguing readings from the *Voyager* crafts indicated an incredibly smooth surface, where significant differences in coloration did not mean corresponding differences in topography. The lines, it was decided, were cracks in the icy surface, where new water—water?—came to fill in the gaps.

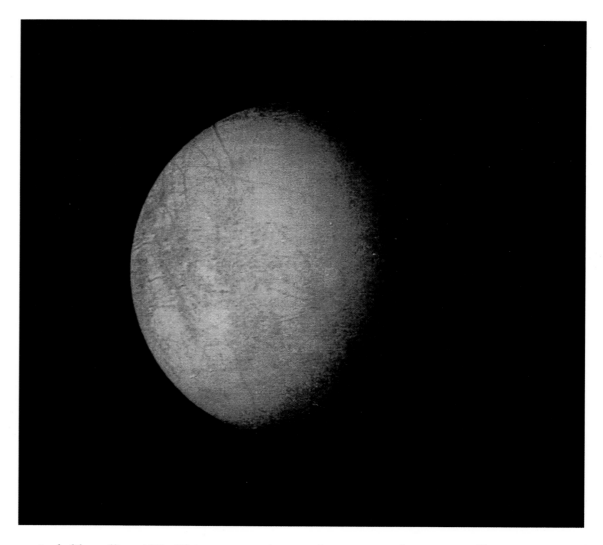

From afar, in this case more than a million kilometers, Europa's color-enhanced image seems vaguely similar to Mars. The regions that appear blue in this photograph are actually white. The picture was taken by Voyager 2 in July of 1979.

And, like yelling "Fire!" in a movie theater, the prospect of water set off an alarm. If the planet's internal core is still keeping things warm enough for liquid water—potentially a good deal of it at that—then doesn't that mean . . . ? The "lifers" were back, and they were keying in on Europa. Internal heat would require a way to vent it—meaning spewing hot molten material into water—which is how many scientists think life on Earth might have been started. This information leaves prognosticators a great future on the "Life of Europa" circuit. While the *Galileo* probe will photograph and survey the moon, it has no way of conducting the necessary tests. Such a mission to Europa is a long way off, as yet unscheduled by any of the currently active space-going nations. Until then the debate is likely to continue.

The discovery of Jupiter's fifth moon, Amalthea, did not occur until 1892, at which time the number of known moons quickly began to climb towards double digits. We now know of four moons orbiting within the Galileans: Amalthea, Thebe, and the two ring shepherds, Adrastea and Metis. Out beyond these eight moons another four rotate alongside them, in sync with

Jupiter's prograde rotation. For this reason alone, we assume the twelve to have been members of the Jovian system since the earliest stages of formation. The fact that the next four or five satellites spin retrograde around Jupiter leads us to believe that they were captured strays from the asteroid belt. How long those objects have been under Jupiter's control remains undetermined.

While Earth-based study of Jupiter continues—and the Hubbell Space Telescope promises long-term, high-resolution tracking of the Jovian atmosphere—close examination remains a long way off. Even if all finally goes well for the jinxed *Galileo* mission, we won't have its data until 1995 or so. Until then we will have to continue digesting all we have learned from the *Voyager* missions. While the answers remain elusive, we're at least getting a better idea of what the next round of questions should be.

Up close, Europa, the smallest of the Galilean moons, reveals a rich network of linear features. The moon was originally thought to have a mantle of ice 100 kilometers thick, but recent theories have postulated a much thinner layer, subject to cracking, which is responsible for its appearance. Voyager 2 captured this image of the moon from 240,000 kilometers away.

SATURN

SATURN, THE RINGED WONDER, IS THE MOST DISTINCTIVE AND PERHAPS THE MOST AWE INSPIRING of all the planets. Since the earliest telescopes were trained upon it, Saturn has done more to capture the imagination of both amateur and professional astronomers than any other planet. An ultralight Gas Giant, it is surrounded by an astonishing assortment of swirling rocks and ice. Its rings and satellites dance around the planet in a rhythm of astonishing complexity. Like the Sun itself, Saturn is the center of its own well-populated neighborhood, a microcosm of the solar system.

Saturn is the second largest planet in the solar system, with a greater mass than the seven smaller members combined. Despite its size, however, Saturn is incredibly light—the least dense of all known planets (with the possible exception of Pluto, for whom specific measurements are hard to determine). Composed primarily of hydrogen and helium, Saturn contains a glimpse into the solar system's past. In exploring its atmosphere and layers of inner liquid, we are given a clue to the composition of the primordial solar nebula. While Jupiter's enormous mass has tampered with much of that matter, cold Saturn has proven to possess better preservative qualities.

Nearly twice as far from the Sun as Jupiter, Saturn receives a quarter as much solar radiation, and it probably had less matter to draw on during its formation. The matter that did collect weighed less, condensed less, and accordingly created less pressure at its center. The result is a cold, gaseous planet lighter than water. (As planetary writers enjoy pointing out, if you could find a lake/ocean/bathtub big enough, Saturn would float. But would it leave a ring?)

If Jupiter occasionally takes a back seat to its satellites, Saturn rides behind in a whole other car. The planet's rings and satellites form a complex system of gravitational and visual wonders far more alluring than the mere planet they revolve around. Galileo's fuzzy observations led him to believe the "planet" was actually a ternary system, with one large planet surrounded by two smaller ones. Over the course of time, however, Galileo watched the system's smaller members diminish and then disappear altogether. In his writings, Galileo wondered if the planet had not reenacted the myth of its namesake, who devoured his young. (A prophesy—one of mythology's great narrative devices—drove Saturn to devour his offspring to prevent them from overthrowing him. Jupiter was spared from his father's murderous hand to emerge as Saturn's successor: king of heaven and earth, sovereign over all gods and mortals.)

Later in the seventeenth century, more sophisticated telescopes revealed the general nature of Saturn's ring. Some astronomers assumed it to be solid, while others had the foresight to imagine a belt of small rocks and debris in close orbit around the planet. The Dutch astronomer, Christiaan Huygens, introduced the idea of the solid ring in a coded anagram added to his pamphlet introducing the first discovery of a Saturnian moon, Titan. At the time of that pamphlet's release in 1656, Huygens believed Saturn's rings to be solid, but he would not publicly commit himself to the belief for another three years. (The anagrams enabled their

Alluring Saturn (opposite page) is seen from Voyager 2's approach to the planet and its moons. The shadow of one of Saturn's moon's, Tethys, can be seen against the planet's light surface.

When Voyager 2 snapped this photo on its approach to Saturn, project scientists were able to discern numerous differences from this image and those taken by its predecessor. The planet's features and rings are color-enhanced, and seen at a distance of nearly fifty-million kilometers.

Saturn's C-ring is turned into a colorful array of subsections in this false-color image taken by Voyager 2 *(opposite page).* **The differences in color indicate variations in the thickness and content of the ring, further subdividing what was thought to be a solid structure.**

creators the opportunity to prove they had already "known" something, without taking the chance of being ridiculed were they to be determined incorrect.) Twenty years later, J.D. Cassini, discoverer of the first subdivision within the rings, proposed the idea of a loose composite ring, introducing the idea of rocks and dust coming together to appear solid from the vast distance of Earth. His theory was not popular with contemporaries, and it fell out of favor for nearly two hundred years.

Sir William Herschel, perhaps the best known figure in the third era of the history of modern astronomy (with the theorists Newton and Kepler representing the first, and Galileo and his contemporaries the second), mistakenly championed the solid-ring theory. Herschel's legacy includes great predictions and discoveries, as well as an equal number of erroneous assumptions. His misguided notions of the nature of Saturn's ring was not unseated until the middle of the nineteenth century. Even the otherwise prescient French cosmologist Laplace went along with the solid-ring theory, but at least he tempered it by breaking the enormous structure into a multitude of subdivided, concentric layers.

A thumbnail sketch of the rings was developed through Earth-based studies, but the finer details have arrived on Earth in the electronic transmissions of three American space probes. *Pioneer 11* was more notable for actually having reached Saturn than for the revelations it provided. It did, however, spot the F-ring and registered a surprisingly powerful magnetic field.

From behind (left), the rings take on a whole new appearance. This photograph shows how the fine particles within the ring scatter the distant sunlight. Taken by Voyager 1 as it moved away from Saturn, this new perspective on its rings forced many scientists to reexamine their theories.

The contrast between front and back views is made particularly apparent when compared with the image above, taken by Voyager 1 before it reached the planet. In all, the first Voyager mission transmitted more than 15,000 images of the planet.

Its path from Jupiter to Saturn was a long trek across the solar system, taking over four years, while the two *Voyagers* that followed closely on its heels needed barely a third of that time. As a result, *Pioneer* preceded the first *Voyager* probe by just one year and served as the equivalent of a sighting scope to the main viewer—scanning the Saturnian system to determine where *Voyager*'s more sophisticated equipment (having been launched four years later and designed to be more complex) should focus. Correspondingly, tests conducted by *Voyager 1* proved particularly helpful in refocusing and refining equipment on *Voyager 2*.

The complexities of the Saturnian system have kept theorists busier than ever in recent years. The more we learn of Saturn's rings, moons, and the planet itself, the more questions we are left with. The success of the Voyager *missions can be gauged by the number of new questions they have inspired.*

The information provided by those missions has added a new dimension to our understanding of Saturn's rings. *Pioneer 11* gave scientists the first opportunity to view the rings when backlit by the Sun. The differences in their coloration indicate varying widths among the rings and suggest an intricate system of subdivisions within them. A *Voyager 2* experiment surprised scientists with its measurement of the light from a distant star as it traveled behind the rings. The early information indicated that no region was totally void of ring particles, though the complete data for that experiment alone will take nearly a decade to process and analyze.

In addition to discerning a greater number of subdivisions among the rings, the *Voyagers* also noticed radial spokes traveling with, and possibly above them. Excited particles, they noticed, formed together across the width of one of the rings. (Unimaginative astronomers dubbed the earliest such portions A-, B- and C-rings.) It's possible that the particles are electrostatically charged as they emerge from behind the planet's shadow, but no one is exactly certain, and any anagrams have yet to be revealed! The spokes break up as the closer particles travel faster than those farther out and as each slowly loses its charge.

As the *Voyager* missions focused on the outer limits of Saturn's ring, they discovered a pair of new moons "shepherding" the particles within the F-ring. Though the fringes of the ring were seen to braid about one another in as many as ten or more "strands," a more startling discovery concerned the next pair of satellites. While the F-ring shepherds (Prometheus and Pandora) simply share the same orbit, Epimetheus and Janus actually swap orbits. Ninety thousand kilometers above the clouds of Saturn, the small satellites play a game of catch-up as they spin around the planet, trading positions every four years.

The more we have learned about the orbits of matter around Saturn, the more we've realized how little we really know. The complex interaction among at least twenty satellites, as well as the considerable mass scattered throughout the rings, defies present explanation. The first seven moons discovered were spotted by the same trio of individuals previously mentioned in regards to the early ring theory: Huygens (1), Cassini (4), and Herschel (2). As with the quickly discovered Galilean moons, these are the largest Saturnian satellites. While the moons Herschel discovered are comparably small, Cassini's are similar in size to those we'll shortly come upon in orbit around Uranus.

Only Titan belongs in the category of the solar system's largest satellites. Recently downgraded to secondary status behind Jupiter's Ganymede, Titan is a hazy world with the

The Saturnian system is the most populous of all, with more moons than there are planets, and a ring more impressive than the asteroid belt. In this composite (opposite page), a number of moons are brought together in their dance about Saturn.

Titan (left) is the largest of Saturn's moons, complete with a thick, hazy atmosphere. In fact, the atmosphere had remained so impenetrable that until scientists became aware of the illusion, the moon was originally thought to be the largest satellite in the solar system.

most substantial atmosphere of any satellite. Larger than Earth's moon, Titan's body was originally thought to be the largest, but the occultation of radio signals from *Voyager 1* as it passed behind Titan indicated a surprisingly thick atmosphere and a correspondingly smaller diameter. What Titan lacks in size, however, it makes up in potential. The planet's photochemical haze is composed primarily of nitrogen, with a good deal of methane mixed in.

Upon interacting with solar radiation, methane is known to create a number of chemical by-products, some of which happen to contain carbon, hydrogen, and oxygen. Combined with Titan's nitrogen atmosphere, their presence establishes the Saturnian moon as the only body besides Earth to contain the four elements essential to the formation of life as we know it. (Methane can also be converted into hydrogen cyanide, a building block of life-forming amino acids.) Unfortunately, however, Titan's average temperature of 95 K (-288°F) makes it unlikely that those elements could be brought together in a way that would lead to the creation of living cells. It's also just a few degrees below the triple-point of methane (temperatures at which a compound can exist in solid, liquid, and gaseous states—such as conditions on Earth that allow water to exist in all three forms), though high atmospheric pressure at the surface may compensate for the difference.

Saturn's moon Enceladus is similar in appearance to Jupiter's Ganymede, but a tenth its size. The tiny satellite is rich in surface features, as illustrated by this photograph taken by Voyager 2 at a distance of 119,000 kilometers.

After considering Titan, the remaining Saturnian moons are a comparatively bland lot, particularly when recalling the diversity of Jupiter's orbital subjects. The four discovered by Cassini—Tethys, Dione, Rhea, and Iapetus—are barren worlds similar to Mercury, the Moon, and Jovian satellites such as Callisto or Ganymede, only smaller. Between a thousand and 1600 kilometers in diameter, all are cratered spheres of rock and ice. Each offers its own idiosyncratic characteristics, but they are easily grouped by all but the most serious planetary observers.

Oddly enough, it is the next size satellite that offers a variety of fascinating features. Mimas, a rock less than four hundred kilometers wide, exhibits an impact crater one third of its diameter. The collision sent shockwaves throughout the moon, like a miniature Caloris Basin, and left a

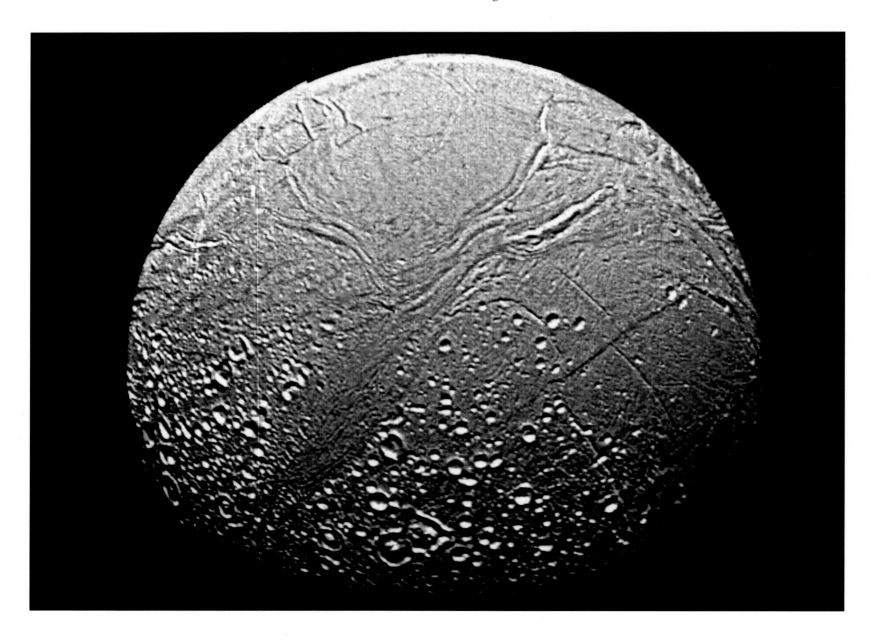

central icy peak ten kilometers above the crater floor—higher than Mount Everest—on a body a minute fraction the size of Earth. (Such peaks are found throughout the solar system. They occur when molten matter—melted by the force of the impact—bounces back from the collision in much the same way slow motion strobe photography of a drop of milk shows a peak rising back up its center just after contact.)

Enceladus, slightly larger than Mimas, contains at least five types of surface features, the most of any of Saturn's satellites with the possible exception of shrouded Titan. This diversity includes rectilinear fault-lines commonly associated with crust movement and features indicative of surface change within the past billion years: a relatively recent occurrence when compared to the dormancy of other distant, frozen worlds.

In sharp contrast, Hyperion is a battered, uneven chunk of rock. Its scarred surface is the oldest in Saturn's system, and it may actually be the largest intact portion of a much larger moon which shattered billions of years ago during the earliest stages of Saturn's formation. Such collisions probably accounted for a good deal of the loose matter that continues to make up Saturn's rings.

Many of Saturn's moons are small objects known as Trojan satellites. The first such Trojans were a pair of asteroids discovered in the orbital path of Jupiter, at distances from the planet in which an equilateral triangle is formed between it, the Sun, and the Trojan. They're known as Langrangian Points, where the Sun and Jupiter exert equal gravitational pull on the object. In the case of Saturn's Trojans, the planet and one of the large moons play the roles of the Sun and Jupiter respectively, with the added complexity of other passing satellites and the mass of the rings. The orbits of these Trojans represent gravitational resonance of incredible intricacy. (It's likely that more satellites, some of them Trojans, will be discovered around 1995-1996, when Saturn's rings are seen edge-on from Earth. At these times, the reflective glare of the rings themselves is eliminated, allowing the barely discernable reflections of such small orbitals to register on photographic plates.)

And finally worth noting is Phoebe, the outcast in Saturn's system. Orbiting the planet in a retrograde motion, Phoebe travels along the solar system's ecliptic plane. All of Saturn's other moons orbit around the planet's equatorial plane in a prograde motion. Taking these facts into consideration, scientists have concluded that Phoebe, like the furthest Jovian satellites (see page 100), is a captured asteroid.

Which leaves Saturn itself, a low-key centerpiece to its impressive surroundings. Much like Jupiter (to whom Saturn is frequently unfavorably compared), Saturn is a ball of hydrogen and helium with a small rocky core at its center. The size of two Earths, Saturn's core accounts for about twenty percent of the planet's mass. The core gives way to liquid metallic hydrogen, though the lower pressures and temperatures than those on Jupiter permit a helium rain to descend through the liquid. As a result, Saturn's atmosphere has a greater proportion of hydrogen to helium than does Jupiter's. The concept of the helium rain is, for the most part, the

creation of scientists seeking to explain the disproportionate amount of hydrogen in Saturn's atmosphere and the unexpected amount of heat radiating from its center. Cold enough to condense and sink towards the planet's center, the helium rain is also credited with giving off thermal energy.

Pioneer 11 discovered a great magnetic field about the planet, whose Van Allen doughnutlike belt cannot begin until it gets past the rings. One reason for its strength is the fact that Saturn's magnetic pole is in almost perfect alignment with its pole of rotation. Instead of spewing out from a twisting spigot, the magnetic energy moves, on its axis, only with the planet's change of seasons. That magnetic pole, like Jupiter's, is inverted from Earth's, meaning that its north is our south and vice versa. (This lends unexpected credence to humorously intended globes and maps placing Antarctica, Australia, etc. "on top" and Europe and "North" America south of the equator.)

The *Voyager* missions provided a great deal of information about Saturn's atmosphere as well, most notably measuring wind speeds in excess of 1800 kilometers per hour. But since Saturn is colder than Jupiter, there is considerably less turbulence than the kind responsible for the Great Red Spot and other Jovian phenomenona. Fine-tuning of *Voyager 2*'s cameras allowed for greater color resolution of Saturn's atmospheric features, but even when enhanced they still paled in comparison to Jupiter.

Scientists are still digesting the wealth of information gathered on Saturn in the last decade. The Hubbell Space Telescope promises to investigate the leads gathered by the *Pioneer* and *Voyager* missions, though any future probes are vague proposals at best. Tentative plans have been developed between NASA and the European Space Agency for a Saturn orbiter (named after Cassini) with a Titan probe, but even if the most optimistic expectations were met, the earliest date such a mission would reach the planet would be the year 2002. When one considers the unfortunate history of the collaboration of those two organizations on the Jovian *Galileo* probe, such optimism seems particularly unfounded.

In the meantime, Saturn remains the beauty of the solar system, easily identified by even the simplest telescopes. Though the body itself remains a scrawny sidekick to mightier Jupiter, its ring is its crowning glory, one of the stunning achievements of planetary creation. Far from the heat of the Sun, deposed Saturn reigns over its remaining loyalists. Miniature moons too numerous to count—no less name—are forever circling the planet's equator, held tightly in their orbits. Like the rings themselves, our understanding of Saturn is scattered and uneven. For centuries it has captured the imagination of all who gazed upon it, and it remains as mysterious and perplexing as ever. One day, earthlings may visit Saturn. Until then, distant Saturn hangs alluringly in the night sky, a testament to the unpredictable wonders of the solar system we occupy in an obscure corner of the Universe.

URANUS

ONE SUN, SIX PLANETS, AND A MOON. FOR THOUSANDS OF YEARS THESE STATISTICS REMAINED unchanged. The solar system was perceived to be a known quantity, its charter members an exclusive lot among the inhabitants of the night sky. With one of the first telescopes, Galileo redefined the order of that system through his discovery of the Jovian moons, but few extrapolated the implications of his heliocentric universe to theorize that other worlds might exist out beyond Saturn. And when the seventh planet was finally discovered, the individual who spotted it failed to realize the historic importance of his actions.

In 1781, an amateur British astronomer, William Herschel, stumbled upon a point of light which displayed a discernible disklike shape. Herschel knew that an ordinary star would not be capable of such an appearance and believed he had discovered some type of comet or nebulous star. The first person in modern times to discover a new world was quite unaware of his accomplishment. Instead, Herschel tracked the object's orbit for a short time and decided it was in fact a new comet. Just visible to the naked eye, the planet had been charted frequently during the century before Herschel's discovery. Others had noted the point of light without tracking its movements over any period of time, simply plotting it as a star. And, were it not for the professional astronomers who realized the actual nature of the "new comet," some other astronomer could easily have displaced Herschel in our histories.

Though our treatment of Herschel here and in other portions of this book may seem a bit harsh, his story is an interesting and occasionally amusing one. His discovery of Uranus came about by accident, while he was searching for a way to measure the distance between the Sun and other stars. He used a homemade telescope whose quality gave Herschel the kind of advantage that fate had bestowed on Galileo, Huygens, and their contemporaries. When others finally enlightened the music teacher as to the true nature of his discovery, Herschel first proposed naming the planet Georgium Sidus in honor of George III, who had named Herschel his personal astronomer and who established a private observatory for him near Windsor Castle. (Herschel would again break tradition by eschewing Greek mythology for British literature when naming his Uranian satellite discoveries for characters found in Shakespeare and Pope.) The remainder of Herschel's life was spent at the cutting edge of planetary science. Though his erroneous predictions have been noted elsewhere, Herschel was a bold thinker who is also credited with having realized that our solar system is itself moving in space—a startling concept at the time.

Herschel would also be credited with having discovered two moons around Uranus (he claimed to have found more but was proved wrong about all but these two), the first of five known prior to the *Voyager 2* mission. Beyond these discoveries, however, the distant world remained a mystery. Earth-based data was sketchy at best, composed of only the most basic information. Scientists eventually established its orbit around the Sun as taking eighty-four years

Uranus, seen (opposite page) in a false-color image taken by Voyager 2 *in 1986, was discovered by William Herschel (above).* **In doing so, Herschel became the first modern individual to discover a new planet.**

(discovering Neptune in the process), but they could only guess that its day was slightly shorter than one on Earth. Visually, the planet offered no clues, as it was shrouded in an aquamarine haze. Its size and density were known, but such numbers are just a small piece in the puzzle of planetary science.

Probably the single most interesting quirk known to scientists was Uranus' wide swing on its axis. At the time of the *Voyager 2* encounter, the planet was essentially spinning on its side, its southern pole pointed towards the Sun. While Earth's twenty-three degree tilt fits comfortably into the planetary norm, Uranus swings more than ninety degrees on its axis. This means a Uranian day at one of the planet's poles lasts forty-two years before slipping into an equally long night. The effects on the planet of this extreme axial movement remain undetermined, as does

the cause for it. Some scientists envision an enormous collision between Uranus and an Earth-sized planetoid early in the planet's history, while those who discount that scenario offer little to replace it.

Orbiting close to the planet's equators, Uranus' moons were only recently found to have a companion in their travels: a series of rings. Until their discovery in 1977, scientists continued to be trapped by the inertia of the past, believing that only Saturn possessed a ring. It was then, during the occultation of a star by the planet, that unsuspecting researchers stumbled upon the discovery of Uranus' rings. The story ranks among the most fascinating of scientific discoveries since World War II—alert individuals realized that they were being shown something they hadn't even known to look for.

American astronomers were trying to determine the depth and content of Uranus' atmosphere by measuring the occulted star as it slipped behind the planet. Having started their recording equipment early to insure that it was working properly, the scientists were surprised to see the star's light waver a number of times before reaching the actual disk of Uranus itself. Their uncertainty and joking turned serious when the pattern was repeated on the other side of the planet after the star reemerged, again registering several dips in intensity before finally clearing the planet's domain. The symmetry of the experiment's results on both sides of the planet could mean only one thing: that Uranus, too, had a ring. This discovery would eventually lead to that of Jupiter's ring and the ringlike arcs around Neptune.

After two centuries of uncertainty, scientists were finally afforded the opportunity to better understand Uranus. Four years after its encounter with Saturn, *Voyager 2* approached the unexplored world of Uranus in January, 1986. Though the visit remains the key to our present knowledge of Uranus, it was by no means ideal. Unlike the leisurely multiorbital encounters of the later probes mentioned in our examination of the terrestrial planets (see page 30), the *Voyager* missions could only enjoy quick fly-bys, like the primitive crafts of the sixties. In the cases of the previously encountered Gas Giants, the *Voyager*s were able to study some satellites during their approach, then focus on the planets themselves during closest proximity, and examine more satellites as they moved off to the next destination. But Uranus would be different.

Spinning on its side, its satellites aligned nearly perpendicular to the ecliptic, the Uranian system was poised like an enormous bull's-eye in space for *Voyager 2* to fly straight through. Having reached its summer solstice in 1985, Uranus was close to its most uncooperative alignment. This meant project scientists needed to create a tight, condensed list of experimental priorities. Key readings were taken during a six hour period that marked the craft's closest approach to Uranus. Cameras spun to record each of the previously known moons: They discovered ten more and a new ring. They focused on the planet when it loomed overhead and then spun around to record its rings backlit, as had been done at Jupiter and Saturn.

One of *Voyager 2*'s most important goals was to finally determine the length of the Uranian day, which it measured at just over seventeen hours. In the process of this rotation, the planet also sprays its magnetic field, like a corkscrew, into space. As if its extreme inclination on its axis were not enough, Uranus' magnetic field is skewed 55° from that deviant pole. (On Earth that would be like having one pole in Los Angeles, the other off the coast of Madagascar.) The solar wind, still strong three billion kilometers away, twists the wild field into a long tail running behind the planet. The constant rocking of the planet from end to end is thought to play a role in the magnetic field's strange relation to Uranus' axis, but some scientists again revert to the collision theory mentioned earlier.

Meanwhile, other team members studying the planet's atmosphere, were perplexed by gales of wind coming out of the west, when everything already known about the atmospheric conditions on Uranus indicated that they should emerge from the east. All that observers had

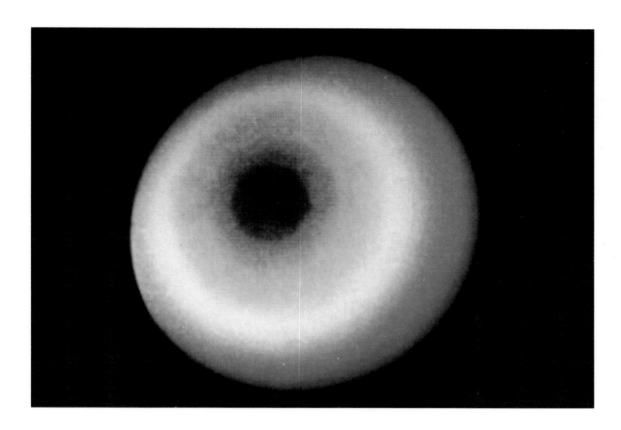

As Voyager 2 approached Uranus in January of 1986, its cameras were forced to contend with diminishing sunlight and a planet fairly uniform in color. The top photo is a false-color image used to detail subtle changes in the planet's atmosphere. The picture below shows how the planet would look to the human eye. In both, the planet's southern pole is located near the center of the hemisphere, it's axis nearly parallel to the ecliptic.

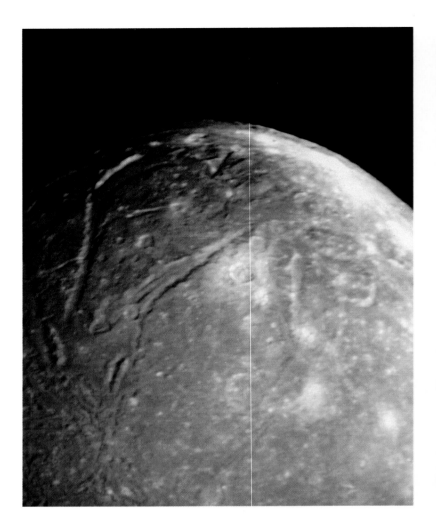

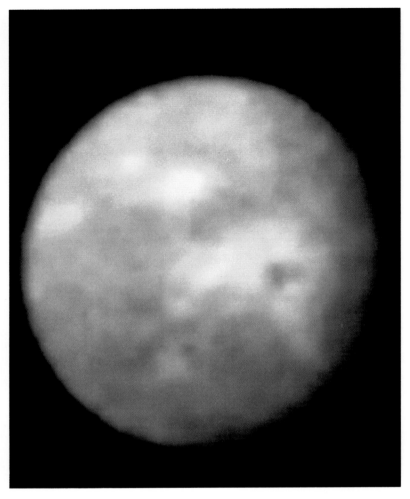

Ariel's complex terrain was captured by Voyager 2 as it sped through the Uranian system (above left). Ariel possesses a number of fairly typical craters, but also includes indications of later geologic activity.

Oberon (above right) is Uranus' outermost satellite. Though variations in color on the planet's surface have led some scientists to theorize about the satellite's history, the resolution of most of the images was insufficient to allow for definite conclusions.

come to expect after encountering Jupiter and Saturn was thrown into disarray as the data began to arrive from Uranus. If Saturn was Jupiter's scrawny companion, Uranus was the odd man out, a perplexing world that could do nothing "right." Its rings were totally different than the others' too—thin bands with great gaps of empty space between them. Nothing was where or what it was supposed to be.

Around the planet's epsilon ring, two of the newly discovered moons were found shepherding material into neat bands. Uranus' rings are noticeably lacking the finer dust found elsewhere; they are composed of large particles ranging in size from small boulders to rocks as big as houses. Having alloted a good deal of precious camera time to backlit photos of the rings, scientists were surprised to find little sign of them. The conditions for ring formation this much farther from the Sun were obviously quite different from those other closer Gas Giants.

The major Uranian moons were also able to befuddle astronomers, who had expected to find long dead worlds frozen solid since the earliest stages of their formation. Two of these moons, however—Ariel and Oberon—both displayed evidence of geologic activity after the initial

Uranus' other two large moons, Titania (above left) and Umbriel (above right), are dark, cratered worlds. Though the Voyager 2 probe passed closer to these moons, it was busy photographing Uranus itself since the entire system was aligned like a bulls-eye through which the craft quickly traveled. The bright ring seen near the top of Umbriel has yet to be explained.

formation of their surfaces. Astronomers were surprised to see plains flooded with younger material and faultlike disruption along major stretches of these small worlds. Both are similar in size to Cassini's discoveries around Saturn (see page 104). Along with Titania and Umbriel, all are between 1100 and 1600 kilometers wide and orbit Uranus at a greater distance than its other known satellites.

The fifth of the previously known moons was tiny Miranda, less than half the size of any of the other four. Despite its diminutive stature, the satellite turned out to be the most interesting of the lot. Offering surface features previously unseen elsewhere in the solar system to date, Miranda proved quite fascinating. It featured extensive fault canyons greater than any on Earth, layered terraces, and a repeating linear pattern that falls somewhere between a trapezoidal racetrack and a poorly ironed kite. Composed of a series of grooves and troughs a few kilometers deep, the features have so far defied any viable explanation.

The idea that a body so small could have undergone such change would have seemed unimaginable a few decades ago. It was clear that any internal energy would quickly dissipate,

Small Miranda emerged as the surprise of the Uranian system. The satellite's chaotic terrain defied the expectations of all astronomers and still remains an unsolved puzzle. This photograph (right) was taken at a distance of 147,000 kilometers by Voyager 2 on January 24, 1986.

An artist's conception of the entire system appears on the opposite page.

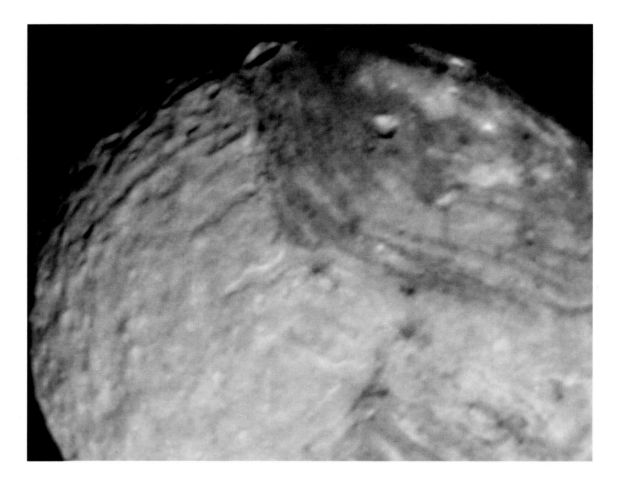

leaving—it was assumed—permanently frozen targets for meteorites and comets. But as physicists and astronomers came to understand the warming effect of planets and neighboring satellites as they pushed and pulled on small moons, it became clear that they could indeed experience geologic activity. This was first shown to be possible during encounters with the Jovian system. It was born out during visits to Saturn. And now Uranus was confounding things again with a satellite that went about the process in a way unlike any other.

Almost as quickly as it arrived at Uranus, *Voyager 2* had passed the planet. It experienced yet another slingshotting into the vast emptiness of space, then another three years of quiescence before approaching its final stop on the itinerary: Neptune. As usual, the visit to Uranus left more questions than answers. The information from the historic encounter will continue to be decoded and disseminated. It will spark debate and foster hypotheses that will go unanswered for a long time to come. It is distinctly possible that we will not see another visit to the distant planet until we are well established in the twenty-first century. It's hard to imagine being around for the next "grand tour alignment"—some time in the early 2160s!—and the prospect of a Uranus-only mission seems unlikely at this time. For now we are left to digest what we have learned and to interpret some small portion of it.

NEPTUNE

WILLIAM HERSCHEL STUMBLED UPON URANUS BY CHANCE. IN DOING SO HE BECAME THE ONLY MAN in modern history to do such a thing. The discovery of Neptune, though more complicated and exacting, did not arrive through the lens of a telescope so much as through the precise calculations of mathematicians. Only by noticing inconsistences in Uranus' orbit did the idea of another, farther planet occur to most skywatchers. Herschel's new planet was a perplexing one, inspiring the search for still another member of the growing solar system.

By the 1840s, sixty years after its discovery, the astronomical community realized that their predictions regarding Uranus' path across the night sky were considerably off. Enough sightings of the planet since its discovery, along with pre-discovery observations that were retrospectively determined to have been of the planet, made it clear that there was an additional force acting on Uranus' orbit. The structure of the then-known solar system could not account for the movement of Herschel's planet.

Though it may receive a bit more attention than it merits, since there is little else to say about the mysterious planet, the story of Neptune's discovery is an interesting one. Two mathematicians—one a recent British graduate, the other a Frenchman unpopular among his peers—predicted the position of the planet almost simultaneously, each unaware of the other's results. John Couch Adams was fresh out of Cambridge's Class of '43 (1843) when he immersed himself in the intricate calculations necessary for such a task. Though he was in fact the first to successfully predict the location of Neptune, his information fell upon deaf ears—particularly those of the Astronomer Royal at the Greenwich Observatory, who was unimpressed with the young upstart.

Urbain Leverrier, the Frenchman, had also completed his calculations and was met with an equal lack of enthusiasm. After encountering resistance from his domestic colleagues, Leverrier eventually sent his data to the Astronomer Royal, George Airy. He compared Leverrier's information with Adams', and realized that it was no coincidence that the two had nearly identical results. Airy instigated a slow, step-by-step search at the best facility in England, the Cambridge Observatory. Ironically, Adams' alma mater had remained deaf to his earlier assertions and was now acting on those of the Frenchman. But the staff at Cambridge was incapable of confirming the planet's existence, having bungled their head start. Leverrier grew frustrated, eventually sending a letter to the Berlin Observatory with his calculations. The night that letter arrived, using a recently obtained star atlas as their guide, the Germans discovered the eighth planet.

Initially, Leverrier was credited as discoverer of the new planet, since it was his work the Germans had employed. John Herschel, Sir William's son and a prominent astronomer himself, helped Adams receive equal billing for the discovery, though it was the Germans who christened

The farthest planet from the Sun, Neptune will be Voyager 2's final stop before hurtling off into unknown space. Seen here in an artist's drawing, the planet was discovered in 1846 as a result of irregularities in the orbit of newly discovered Uranus.

the new planet. It was the Germans who had actually seen the planet's blue-green disk, maintaining the mythological tradition by selecting Neptune, god of the oceans, son of Saturn.

Today, very little is known about Neptune, its satellites, and its potential ring. *Voyager 2* speeds towards the planet for a rendezvous in late summer, 1989, at which time scientists will learn much more about the distant world than they have in the hundred-plus years since its discovery. Presently, however, Neptune is perceived as a near twin to Uranus, slightly smaller in diameter though greater in mass. Both are balls of gas with rocky cores at their center. They have deep oceans and atmospheres of hydrogen and methane. Neptune, however, is fifty percent farther from the Sun than Uranus, which led scientists to assume that it would be considerably colder. Eventually, however, they came to see that it was only two degrees colder than Uranus. This indicated that Neptune was creating heat internally. Considering how similar the planet is to Uranus—which is not believed to generate any appreciable internal heat itself—this finding came as a surprise to scientists.

Through a telescope, distant Neptune is equal in size to Jupiter's Ganymede. Galileo himself is believed to have spotted the planet without recognizing its true nature, but even those who know this have learned little more about the planet. Its period of rotations remains a mystery, estimated at somewhere between 17.7 and 19.6 hours. Though it is certain that Neptune takes 165 years to circle the Sun, scientists have yet to follow a complete orbit. The planet will not return to the point in the sky where German astronomers first found it until 2011.

In addition to finally determining the length of Neptune's day, *Voyager 2* also hopes to solve the riddle of Neptune's ring. Shortly after the discovery of Uranus' ring, astronomers began a search for rings around the other Gas Giants. Jupiter tested positive, but Neptune offered a new set of challenges. In May of 1981, astronomers were provided with the first favorable occultation (the passing of a star behind a body, allowing astronomers to determine the size and speed of that body) of a star by Neptune to determine if the planet possessed a ring. The initial results were disappointing. However, a similar test in 1984 sparked some optimism and led to a reevaluation of earlier readings. Present theory involves a series of arcs traveling around the planet like an incomplete ring. While some scenarios involve clearly defined separations between the arcs, it seems more likely that *Voyager 2* will reveal a more continuous ring, with some regions of greatly concentrated matter and others considerably sparser. If we've learned anything from hundreds of years of planetary theory, it's that few things hold hard and fast but seem to blend slowly and intricately to create effects easily simplified.

At present we are aware of two Neptunian moons, and possibly a third. The first, Triton, was discovered shortly after the planet itself by a brewer from Liverpool, England, William Lassell. He had managed to spot a satellite slightly larger than Jupiter's Io or Earth's Moon, wide and bright enough to reflect the Sun's distant light back through the amateur astronomer's lens. Triton spins rapidly around Neptune, orbiting every five days. Since it circles Neptune in a retrograde motion, its orbit is actually a descending one. Just as Earth's Moon will one day escape from its orbit, Triton will spiral slowly inward until it collides with Neptune. Such a spectacle would surely be exciting and informative, but it remains tens of millions of years into the future.

Unlike rapidly moving Triton, Neptune's only other presently known companion takes a full year to circle the planet. Nereid is a tiny ball of ice and rock that remained unnoticed until 1949. It was discovered by Gerard Kuiper, one of this century's greatest astronomers. Kuiper had already discovered Titan's atmosphere, the presence of carbon dioxide on Mars, and Uranus' fifth moon, Miranda, before identifying Nereid. Beyond the fact that it does exist, however, we know little of the tiny satellite, some three hundred kilometers in diameter.

A third moon was announced in 1981, but official confirmation will only come with the arrival of *Voyager 2*. Given the nature of Neptune and the numerous satellites revealed by the *Voyager* missions around the inner Gas Giants, it seems likely that the number of known Neptunian moons will rise sharply in the near future.

In fact, all that we know about Neptune will dramatically increase in the near future. As it did with Uranus, *Voyager 2* will, we hope, reveal fascinating new details of a distant world. The last visit on NASA's grand accomplishment will bring the craft to within 3,000 kilometers of the planet, before hurling it out into distant space. *Voyager 2* will have to contend with rapidly dwindling lighting, twelve years of travel over billions of kilometers, and the trick of passing its data back across that distance to Earth. Radio telescopes, such as the Very Large Array in the deserts of New Mexico, will strain to tune in *Voyager 2*'s weak signals. Those radio messages, traveling at the speed of light, will take four hours to reach Earth, and if both ends do their jobs right we will soon know much more about enigmatic Neptune.

Tom Carroll/FPG Intl.

With "ears" pointed upwards, scientists await the stream of data that will flow across billions of kilometers of space as Voyager 2 encounters Neptune. Since the probe's launch, advances in radio telescope technology have made it possible to learn more about the distant world than had been imagined.

This artist's rendering shows the sketchy view we have of Pluto and its moon. Little detail is included since little is known about the small, distant, frozen world.

PLUTO

PLUTO IS A PLANET. IT ORBITS THE SUN, AND HAS AN ATMOSPHERE AND A MOON OF ITS OWN. Whether it has always been a planet is uncertain. Where it might have come from and how it got there are equally uncertain. When you get right down to it, very little about distant Pluto *is* certain. It was not discovered until well into this century, after a long, painstaking search of billions of light images on an extensive series of photographic plates.

The search for Pluto was begun around the turn of the twentieth century, when astronomers realized that Neptune alone could not explain the deviations in Uranus' orbit. Another planet, they reasoned, must exist farther beyond the newest discovery. William Pickering, a former colleague of Mars-struck Percival Lowell, first proposed a ninth planet in 1908, publishing more detailed information in 1919 about "Planet 0."

Lowell had in the meantime arrived at a similar conclusion, and the two embarked on separate searches for what both assumed would be another Gas Giant far from the Sun. Lowell failed to detect such a giant in a series of long-exposure photographs taken in 1915, though later reexamination revealed dim Pluto on two of the plates. After Pickering's publication, the Mount Wilson Observatory in California (now known as one of the Hale Observatories along with Palomar Mountain) conducted a similar search, and it also failed to detect the diminutive planet that was, it turned out, on a number of these exposures too.

The search died down for a number of years, until the revitalized Lowell Observatory emerged from an estate suit initiated by Lowell's widow. One of Lowell's nephews took charge of the observatory, and renewed the search for "Uncle Percy's Planet." To orchestrate the search he brought in an enthusiastic amateur from Kansas, Clyde Tombaugh. Tombaugh would spend the next few years examining millions of star images with a blink comparator, a device used to compare photographic plates to determine if any images are moving in relation to the neighboring stars. In February of 1930, using plates taken six nights apart the month before, Tombaugh discovered Pluto.

Of the thousands of suggested names that flooded the Lowell Observatory, Tombaugh & Co. chose Pluto, king of the underworld. It's probably no coincidence, however, that the choice featured the initials of Percy Lowell as its first two letters, which were combined to form the planet's shorthand symbol as well.

Pluto's moon was discovered in 1978. That satellite, Charon, is more than half the size of its partner, creating more of a binary system than a planet-moon relationship such as those of the other Gas Giants. Charon orbits close to the planet, a mere 19,000 kilometers from its surface. As a result, some theories consider the moon a fractured piece of a larger, single planet, while others see it as another Neptunian satellite—along with Pluto—before the two were driven from the planet's control. It is possible, however, that the two formed together in their own eccentric orbit. We know that they are locked into a geostationary orbit, where each hovers above the

Percival Lowell, 1855–1916, was an amateur astronomer wealthy enough to build his own observatory. Though Lowell himself was a firm believer in the existence of life on Mars, his greatest legacy remains the discovery of Pluto, in his name, fourteen years after his death.

same point on the other, tumbling and twisting in a wide loop around the Sun. Perhaps their similar masses and great proximity to one another are responsible for their exaggerated orbit.

Pluto is believed to be some 2400 kilometers in diameter, much smaller than Earth's Moon or the other large satellites. It's half the size of the next smallest planet, Mercury, and has one thirtieth of Mercury's mass. This means that Pluto has the lowest density of any of the solid planets, very close to that of water. As a result, scientists assume the planet is primarily composed of water ice, with some methane at its surface. A debate has arisen recently about whether the methane detected on Pluto's surface is the sign of a tenuous atmosphere or simply indicates the presence of methane frost.

From Pluto, the Sun is a dim light in the sky, providing the kind of illumination a full Moon reflects to the Earth. At this point in time the planet appears larger than it has in nearly 248 years, the length of Pluto's orbit around the Sun. Until the turn of the next century, in fact, Pluto will be closer to the Sun than Neptune, normally considered the eighth planet. Pluto's orbit, astronomers quickly realized, is the most elliptical of all the planets and deviates most from the ecliptic plane. Since 1979 Pluto has been closer to the Sun, and it will continue to be until March of 1999. From its perihelion at 4.4 billion kilometers, Pluto will then swing out to the farthest known reaches of the solar system, eventually 7.3 billion kilometers out.

With Pluto's relative proximity to the Sun, contemporary astronomers had hoped to get a closer look at the planet. Original plans for the Grand Tour, a proposal that would eventually be whittled down to the *Voyager* missions, included a third probe that would visit Jupiter and Saturn before veering off for Pluto. Favorable alignments for such a mission occur every twelve years, the length of Jupiter's orbit, since the giant planet is needed to slingshot such a probe across vast distances. As Pluto continues to move away from the Sun, each successive opportunity will prove less appealing. Unless a mission can be mounted for 2001, it seems highly unlikely a visit to the receding world will take place during the early part of the twenty-first century.

Without any visits to the ninth planet, we are unlikely to learn much about it. Conditions on other worlds and improved Earth-based observations can slightly enlighten us about some things, but it seems likely that the biggest questions will remain unanswered for a long time. The kinks in Pluto's orbit have yet to be understood (one complete trip around the Sun will not have been charted until the twenty-second century), and the planet is currently in the midst of a five-year period of Earth-visible eclipses with its moon. From these observations astronomers hope to add greater detail to our sketchy picture of Pluto, but a fully realized understanding remains beyond the foreseeable future. The first breakthrough derived from these observations involved the possibility that Pluto's tenuous atmosphere extended to envelop the planet's moon. Though such an atmosphere is a far cry from that which surrounds most other planets, these theories present new insight to our understanding of this distant world. Cold Pluto, sitting quietly at the edge of the known solar system, remains an elusive outcast from the brotherhood of orbiting bodies—the last outpost of man's planetary understanding.

Beyond Pluto: A Tenth Planet?

OF COURSE THERE'S A TENTH PLANET. ISN'T THERE? AN INEVITABLE DISCOVERY IN THE MINDS OF some remains elusive despite increasingly detailed searches conducted by increasingly sophisticated equipment. If such a planet does indeed exist, it has probably been recorded by one of these searches, particularly the IRAS (Infrared Astronomy Satellite) survey conducted in 1983. The IRAS recorded millions of heat sources during its search, and the tenth planet—if it exists— is included in that experiment's enormous volume of data. As a result, it is possible that some time over the course of the next few years, project scientists will arrive at a heat source that moves faster than those emanating from distant stars. At that point, a new member of the solar system will be named.

Given the secondary status of diminutive Pluto, it is possible that any further world would be equally scrawny and questionable. The presence of another Gas Giant has almost certainly been proved impossible, to the point where scientists can safely say that no such object orbits the Sun within twenty billion kilometers. (That's seven times the distance of Neptune to the Sun.)

It is possible, however, that a smaller, solid body orbits the Sun beyond the path of Pluto. Such a planet could have an effect on the path of the space probes that have already traveled past their primary destinations. Scientists continue to watch *Pioneer 10,* which will reach a distance of two times farther than Pluto's semimajor axis around the year 2001, in hope of detecting such a change in its course. If detected, such movement will probably also be claimed as proof of a binary companion to the Sun, such as Nemesis. Meanwhile, Earth-bound astronomers continue to search the skies for a glint of motion among the dimmest stars—the slight, telltale movement of tenth planet. So far their searches have gone unrewarded.

VOYAGER 2: YOU CAN GET THERE FROM HERE

THE ALIGNMENT OF THE GAS GIANTS THAT GRACED THE *VOYAGER 2* MISSION IS BY NO MEANS A frequent occurrence. The last time such a favorable order existed Thomas Jefferson was President; the next one will not occur until the twenty-second century. The long orbits of these enormous planets create a rhythm which only occurs once every 175 years. At such times, a launched probe such as the *Voyager 2* would be able to ricochet from one world to the next, gaining enough speed in the process to fling it across increasingly vast portions of interplanetary space.

While the precise dance of the planets was essential for *Voyager 2* project scientists even to consider exploring Uranus and Neptune, it was their ingenuity and expertise that made the trip a reality. Team members would eventually have to deal with a mechanical malfunction, photographic conditions exponentially more difficult than those encountered at Jupiter and Saturn, a failed radio receiver (whose backup was itself partially crippled), and the need to accelerate data

From NASA's Jet Propulsion Laboratory's Deep Space Network, information is received from the distant Voyager 2 probe. (A test model is seen on the opposite page.) As information about Neptune reaches such stations, a new surge of activity and interest will be under way.

transmission. Each problem necessitated its own solution, most running contrary to the programs with which *Voyager 2* had been launched nearly a decade earlier.

The most important difference of the Uranian encounter would be the drastic reduction in available sunlight. Twice as far from the Sun as Saturn, which was itself twice the distance of Jupiter, Uranus received one-sixteenth of the illumination as the king of planets. These conditions meant cameras would need longer exposures in order to photograph the unknown planet and its moons. If such lengthy exposures were attempted while the craft's original programs were intact, correction for drift and the operation of other equipment would result in blurred, essentially useless, pictures. In addition to "fooling" *Voyager*'s onboard systems, programmers also had to take into account the deterioration of an actuator responsible for positioning the probe's scanning platform. Experiments with mock-ups of the *Voyager* craft here on Earth, and similar tests performed on *Voyager 1* now flying out of the solar system in search of the heliopause (the point at which the solar wind gives way to interstellar wind), provided a solution but limited the speed at which the platform could be moved.

Before launch, Voyager 2 was outfitted with numerous special features, including a record titled "Sounds of Earth." The gold-plated record offers an aural introduction to our planet to any life forms that may eventually come upon the probe.

In addition, transmissions from the craft were simplified, enabling it to pass along greater amounts of data, though increasing the chance of garbled messages. The leading culprit was the camera again, which was able to transmit photographs composed of 640,000 separate units (pixels), capable of registering 256 levels of brightness. The result was a message needing over five million bits of information to get itself across. Having finally found a way of cutting that amount in half without an appreciable loss of resolution, project members must have been particularly miffed by the blotches that appeared on photographs of Uranus six days before the craft's encounter with it. A quick patch was inserted into the craft's program banks, permitting the subsequent transmission of over 6,000 photos of the mysterious planet and its moons.

The *Voyager* probes are integral to our understanding of the Gas Giants. Two small crafts hurled into the farthest reaches of our solar system have maintained their electronic chatter across billions of kilometers, and could continue to do so well into the next century. *Voyager 2*'s encounter with Neptune in 1989 will be its final and perhaps greatest challenge. Even if that encounter were a total failure, the *Voyager* missions would remain among the most important achievements of mankind's space exploration to date.

SOURCES FOR FURTHER READING

Couper, Heather with Nigel Henbest, *New Worlds: In Search of the Planets.* Reading, Massachusetts: Addison-Wesley Publishing Company, Inc., 1985.

Ghitelman, David, *The Space Telescope.* New York: B. Mitchell, 1987.

Greeley, Ronald, *Planetary Landscapes.* London: Allen & Unwin, 1985.

Holy Bible, King James Version. Cleveland: The World Publishing Company.

Meszaros, Stephen Paul, *Photographic Catalog of Selected Planetary Size Comparisons.* Washington, D.C.: NASA Technical Memorandum, 1985.

Mitton, Jacqueline, *Astronomy.* New York: Charles Scribner's Sons, 1978.

NASA, *The Voyager Flights to Jupiter and Saturn.* Washington, D.C.: U.S. Government Printing Office, 1982.

Pasachoff, Jay M., *Astronomy: From the Earth to the Universe.* Philadelphia: Saunders College Publishing/CBS College Publishing, 1987.

Powers, Robert M., *Mars: Our Future on the Red Planet.* Boston: Houghton Mifflin, 1986.

Strom, Robert G., *Mercury: The Elusive Planet.* Washington, D.C.: Smithsonian Institution Press, 1987.

Trefil, James S., *Space Time Infinity.* New York: Pantheon/Smithsonian Books, 1985.

Weiner, Jonathan, *Planet Earth.* New York: Bantam Books, 1987.

Whipple, Fred L., *Orbiting the Sun: Planets and Satellites of the Solar System.* Cambridge, Massachusetts: Harvard University Press, 1981.

INDEX

H

Hall, Asaph, 76
Harriot, Thomas, 60
Helium, on Saturn, 113–114
Herschel, John, 126
Herschel, William, 80, 104, *117*, 126
 Uranus discovered by, 117
Hubbell Space Telescope, *21*
 Jupiter to be studied with, 101
 Saturn to be studied by, 115
Hurricanes, on Earth, *53*
Hutton, James, 54
Huygens, Christiaan, 103
Hydrogen
 on Jupiter, 90
 on Saturn, 113–114
Hyperion (Saturnian moon), 113

I

Infrared Astronomy Satellite (IRAS), 133
Io (Jovian moon), *91*
 characteristics of, 97–98
 volcanic activity on, 90, *96, 98*

J

Journey to the Moon, A (Verne), 60
Jupiter, 88–101
 asteroids affected by, 83
 atmosphere of, 92–95
 comparative size of, 90
 composition of, 90
 Great Red Spot on, 92, *92, 93*
 heat convection on, 95
 heliocentric solar system and, 90
 magnetic field of, 98
 magnetosphere of, 92
 mass and pressure of, 90
 moons of. *See* Moons (Jupiter)
 polar region, 92

ring around, 95
rotation of, 92
size of, 89

K

Kant, Immanuel, 14
Kepler, Johannes, 76
Kuiper, Gerard, 129

L

Langrangian Points, 113
Laplace, Pierre Simon, 14, 104
Lassell, William, 128
Leverrier, Urbain, 34, 126
Lomonsov, Mikhail, 42
Lovelock, James, 56
Lowell, Percival, 68, *131*
 Pluto's discovery and, 131
Luna probes, 22, 60, 62
Lyot, Bernard, 27

M

McDivitt, James, *58–59*
Magellan probes, 47
Mangala Vallis (Mars), *74*
Mariner probes, 22
 Mars studied by, 68
 Mercury studied by, 35–39
 solar orbit of, 38
 Venus passed by, 43
Marius, Simon, 90
Mars, 66–79
 Ascreaus Mons on, *71*
 atmosphere of, 69
 belief in life on, 68
 ''canals'' on, 68

channels on, *73*
Chryse Planitia on, *69*
dust storms on, 73
existence of life disproved, 72
Mangala Vallis on, *74*
moons of. *See* Moons (Mars)
Olympus Mons on, 66, *72*
polar caps of, 72–73
projected manned exploration of, 78–79
proximity to Earth of, 78
surface of, 66, 68, 69, *69*
temperature of, 74–75
Tharsis Bulge on, 66
Valleris Marineris on, 68, *71*
volcanic activity on, *66*
water on, 73–75
Mars probes, 68–69
Mathematics, Neptune discovered using, 126
Mercury, 32–39
 atmosphere of, 38–39
 Caloris Basin on, 37
 iron core of, 37–38
 magnetic field of, 37
 moon compared with, 32–33
 orbit of, 33–34
 rotation and length of day, 34–35
 scarps on, 37–38, *39*
 surface of, *32–33*
 volcanic activity on, 37
 Weird Terrain of, 37
Meteorites, 83
Methane, on Pluto, 132
Mimas (Saturnian moon), 112–113
Miranda (Uranian moon), *124*
 characteristics of, 123–124
Moon (Earth), 60–65
 atmosphere of, 64
 distance from Earth, 60
 Earth affected by, 57
 Earth's proximity to, *60–61*
 first landing on, 60
 first manned landing on, 60, *62*
 gravitational interlock and, 63
 orbit of, 62–63
 origination of, 62
 role in solar eclipses of, 26